The TWELVE GHOSTS of CHRISTMAS

Tom Slemen

The Tom Slemen Press

Copyright © 2013 Tom Slemen

All rights reserved.

ISBN-10: 1503373835
ISBN-13: **978-1503373839**

IN MEMORIAM

Alvin Stardust
(1942-2014)

CONTENTS

Introduction	1
Hag Night	12
The Missing Room	22
The Christmas Ghost Ship	31
A Christmas Exorcism	42
Tinsel and Timeslips	64
Bobby	86
The Christmas Ball	97
The Singers	112
Truth Be Told	124
The Red Man	130
Crystal Clear	146
The Last Christmas	161

INTRODUCTION

Before you read of the Twelve Ghosts of Christmas may I tell you a few eerie stories of the festive season that have stuck in my mind over the years?

Planted over a millennia ago, the 90,000-acre New Forest of Hampshire is one of England's few remaining unspoiled tracts of land. Two thirds of it are open to the public, but long ago this vast verdant treasure was the royal hunting preserve of William the Conqueror, and such an ancient place is bound to have its ghosts. As recently as 2012, the eerie solid-looking ghost of a man in a large dark leather hood – similar to that of an executioner's hood – was seen by many tourists in the New Forest on horseback, with a long bow strung across his back. He's thought to be a poacher who was put to death for killing a deer in Medieval times under the Draconian Norman laws. The Normans protected the game of their forests with notorious ferocity, and anyone found killing a deer was sentenced to death, and should the person steal the deer he would have his hands chopped off at the wrists or slowly sawn off. Attempted theft of a deer or disturbing the animal resulted in the budding poacher being blinded. These harsh sentences were eventually mitigated and the Plantagenet kings were far more lenient towards poaching. Richard the Lionheart eventually abolished the death penalty for poaching and also put an end to offenders having their hands amputated and their eyes being gouged out (or burst with a glowing poker tip) – but the mob law of village vigilantes towards alleged witches in this area could be just as wicked as the Norman penalties. In the 1960s, a 30-year-old Hampshire teacher named Cathy took her 5-year-old son Robert and 11-year-old niece Gale out one snowy morning on Christmas Eve for a walk in the New Forest to gather wood for the fire and to see the wintry splendour of nature. Robert wanted to feed the birds, and so he carried a little brown paper bag full of bread crumbs, and Gale wanted to see a robin.

Cathy and the children heard strange sounds when they were out collecting wood, and the teacher thought it sounded like someone mute trying to speak. She and her son and niece went cautiously to the source of the sounds and came upon the stuff of nightmares.

Two naked girls, aged perhaps seventeen or eighteen, were leaning with their bloody faces against the trunk of a large old oak, and both girls had their hands tied behind their back. Little Robert began to cry when he saw the blood streaming down the chins of the girls, and Cathy went to their aid and asked them what had happened as she looked about – for she had an intense feeling of being watched.

The girls could not reply to the teacher's questions because their tongues had been nailed to the tree. Each tongue had two broad-headed black nails through it. The only way they could have freed themselves was by ripping their tongues away from the bark – and neither was prepared to do that. Cathy could see the tears streaming down the faces of the girls, and she promised she'd go and get help. Cathy and her sobbing son and Gale hurried away and the teacher made a mental note of the surroundings so she'd know the way back when she found help. Perhaps she'd find a ranger, she thought, but wondered if any would be around on Christmas Eve.

'Who did that to them, auntie?' Gale kept asking, her eyes bulging with fear as she kept glancing back towards the teens.

'Come on, Gale, we'll find someone,' Cathy urged her niece, and she picked up Robert and said, 'There, there, Robert, it's alright, it's alright.' The teacher could not help fearing that the psychopath who had bound the wrists of those girls and nailed their tongues to a tree might now be following her and the children.

'There's a man, auntie!' Gale pointed to a tall square-shouldered man of about fifty who was walking along a path about a hundred yards away. He wore a brown tweed jacket, ochre trousers and Wellingtons and wore a chequered flat cap. He had a black Labrador dog with him, and he slowed down when he saw Cathy and the children.

'Excuse me!' Cathy shouted to the stranger and she put Robert down for a moment as she waved with both hands.

The man came over towards her, and as he did the schoolteacher could see he had white hair sprouting out from the sides of his cap.

'Yes?' he said and his dog ran to Gale, wagging its tale.

Cathy told him about the naked girls tied up and nailed to the tree by their tongues, and the man reacted by exhibiting a nervous tic in his cheek. He didn't seem at all as shocked as Cathy expected he would.

'Ah, with their hands tied behind their back – ' he said, and averted his gaze.

'Yes!' Cathy picked up a hysterical Robert again and then wondered how the middle-aged man knew this. A terrible thought flashed across her mind: was he the psychopath who had committed this evil deed?

'Well, they've been seen before – many times – over the years,' the man said, and he looked at Cathy with a grave expression. 'They're ghosts, you see, miss, they're not real, like.'

Cathy was speechless as she patted Robert on the back.

'Ghosts?' Gale asked, and looked at her auntie as if she'd expand on what the man had just said.

'Look, I'll show you,' the man said, and he walked in the direction of the oak where the girls had been seen. He explained along the way that he was from the nearby village of Minstead, and had lived in the area for fifty-five years. 'There are some queer things seen in the Forest,' he said, and he walked and talked about ghosts of highwaymen, spectres of kings and of the many werewolves that were said to roam the heaths, bogs, farmlands and hamlets of the immense forest. 'These girls are the ghosts of two witches they say,' said the man from Minstead, 'and that's how they punished some of them in those days. When the witch uttered spells to harm, they sometimes cut her tongue out, but if she was young they'd pin their tongues to an oak.'

He stopped talking about further gruesome acts of long ago when he realised young Gale was listening, and he pointed to the old oak where, just a few minutes ago, Cathy and the children had witnessed the barbaric scene which would live forever in their memories. There were no girls there now. The brown paper bag of breadcrumbs Robert had dropped when he saw the moaning girls was still there, lying in the snow.

'See? Not a soul there, miss.' The stranger pointed to the oak, and called back his Labrador as it headed for the tree.

'Oh Lord,' Cathy said, shaking her head slightly. 'We saw them plain as day, didn't we? She turned to look at Gale, and Gale nodded.

'They always see them around this time of year, always round Christmas,' the man said, and then he whistled to his dog, which once again headed for the oak, and then he accompanied Cathy from the area and she went home with Gale and Robert, and that night, all three of them had nightmares about the tortured ghosts.

There is an ancient widespread tradition which says that ghosts are specifically prohibited from putting in an appearance on Christmas Day, supposedly because the Saviour was born upon that day, but the data I have on ghosts contradicts this belief, for many ghosts appear at Christmas. The origins of the belief that ghosts dare not walk on Christmas stem from the misconception surrounding the birthday of Jesus Christ, which was not December 25th. The Bible states that the shepherds were watching their flocks at night when Jesus was born in Bethlehem, but the weather in Judea in December is exceptionally cold and rainy and the shepherds would have found shelter for their sheep. Furthermore, the Bible mentions the Romans taking a census at the time of Jesus' birth, and the Romans never took a census in the winter when temperatures would have been sub-zero and the roads and highways would have been in a treacherous condition. Even prominent Biblical scholars have suggested that Jesus was probably born not in December but in the late summer or early autumn. It was most likely the end of September, because the mother of John the Baptist – Elizabeth – was six months' pregnant when Jesus was conceived, so we can determine the rough date when Jesus was born if we can establish just when John the Baptist was born. John's father was a priest named Zacharias, who served in the Temple in Jerusalem during the term of Abijah (which lasted from June 13 to June 19), and during this period, Zacharias learned his wife would be having a child, so assuming that the conception of John took place at the end of that June, adding nine months brings us to the birth of the Baptist – the end of March, and if we then add another six months (the age difference between John and Jesus) we establish that Jesus was born at the end of September. So why is Christmas (originally called Christ's Mass, or *Cristemasse* in Middle English) marked as the annual commemoration of the birth of Jesus Christ then? In 274 C.E. the Roman Emperor Aurelian decreed that a feast of the birth of the Unconquered Sun (Sol Invictus, the Roman Sun God) should be held each year on 25 December, and this date was chosen because the pagans of old marked that day in their own calendar, possibly with rites connected to the observance of the Winter Solstice and a solar festival with origins lost in the mists of time. When

Christianity arrived in Western Europe, and Britain in particular, the early church unashamedly hijacked the dates of the pagan and Druid festivals and renamed them Easter and Christmas. Even Samhain (Halloween) had All Souls Day placed upon it. So, the old tradition about Christmas being a ghost-free period is shown to have no religious basis whatsoever. In fact, many ghosts are said to appear specifically on Christmas Day, such as the apparition of Anne Boleyn which has been seen to appear under the huge oak tree where she courted Henry VIII at Hever Castle in Kent. Anne's ghost lingers under the boughs of the ancient tree before walking in silence across a bridge which spans the River Eden in the castle grounds. Pausing on the bridge to gaze into the water, Anne tosses a sprig of holly into the river before slowly fading away. Another royal connection to the spirit world is Buckingham Palace, where many of the ghosts tend to become active at Christmastime for various reasons. The solid-looking phantom of a former coachman named Henry Fricker, who on the Saturday night of 11 November 1837, hanged himself by his long silk handkerchief at a room in Buckingham Palace, prefers to walk from Christmas Eve to Boxing Day. Another Christmas ghost at the palace is said to be Francis Norton, who once held a high position in the Royal Kitchen until he decided, for reasons unknown, to cut his throat from ear to ear one afternoon in 1854. In the early hours of Christmas morning of that year he was seen in the Royal Kitchen, apparently supervising the cooks as they boiled the Christmas puddings and iced the Christmas cakes, and he is said to still put in the occasional seasonal appearance, as is Major John Gwynne, the personal secretary to King Edward VII who decided to blow his brains out one Christmas at the beginning of the 20th Century. Gwynne had been depressed over his treatment from friends and society as a whole because he had divorced his wife. On many occasions, always at Christmas, Royal security men at Buckingham Palace have sprung into action after hearing the sound of a single gunshot which always seems to come from a certain room on the first floor of the palace. This was the room Major Gwynne took his life in all those years ago.

From Royalty I come down to earth a little, to a humble working class mystery of the unknown which I recall from many Christmases ago. In 1999, a 50-year-old woman named Karen Thompson visited me one afternoon in the reception area of a radio station I had just been featured on talking about the supernatural. Karen was a secretary for a firm of solicitors, and had never really entertained the idea of ghosts and the paranormal. She struck me as a very down to earth woman, but she had a strange tale to tell. In December 1998 she finally patched up her differences with her younger sister Kelly. They'd had a silly falling out five years before and had hardly spoken to one another during that time, but one day, just a week before Christmas 1998, Karen had decided to patch up her differences with Kelly, and so she decided to buy her sister an expensive pair of gold earrings that she knew Kelly had always wanted. These earrings were almost £250 but money was no object to Karen when she loved someone and she so desperately wanted to build a bridge to her sister after five years of being apart from her. After all, when they were kids, Karen had always looked after her kid sister and as she got older the memories of their days together seemed more precious.

The sisters made an arrangement to meet on Christmas Eve at a restaurant in Manchester, but then tragedy struck. Kelly had a bad asthma attack days before the arranged meeting and sadly died. Karen was devastated and at first she went to throw the gold earrings in the bin, but her husband told her not to do that, and said she should put them on Kelly in her coffin. Karen screamed at him and said it was a morbid suggestion but when she eventually calmed down, she thought it would be a fitting gesture, and so, when a wake was held at Kelly's house, Karen had to hold back a flood of tears as she put the earrings on her sister as she lay in the coffin. 'I love you so much,' she told her sister, 'and I always will love you, sis.'

When the wake had ended the coffin lid was screwed down and Kelly was interred in a graveyard just outside of Liverpool.

On Boxing Day, Karen was dangerously drunk. She had tried to numb her heartache by drinking over Christmas Eve and Christmas Day, but she still found herself breaking down now and then when she thought about those stupid five years she'd been apart from her little sister. Her husband took her up to bed and stroked her head as he sat at the side of the bed, telling her she'd be okay and that Kelly was now with Jesus. Karen fell fast asleep, and she had a very strange dream. She dreamt the she was in bed – in the very bed she was actually asleep in – and the bedroom door opened slowly all by itself, and sunlight blazed in through the doorway. A silhouette appeared in the glare, and it was a familiar outline. It was Kelly, and she looked exactly as she had when Karen had last set eyes on her five years back. She came over to the bed and smiled. 'I've come back for a bit, Karen,' Kelly said, and her voice had a slight echo to it.

'But Kelly, you're dead,' Karen said, and started to sob as she held her arms out.

'No, I'm not, and I've come back to tell you to stop crying. I'm with the Lord now, and its beautiful where I am. I know you feel bad because we were apart for so long but it's alright now, because I'll always be in your heart and you'll always be in my heart.'

Karen then noticed the earrings, and smiled.

'They're lovely Karen, thanks,' Kelly said, and she felt one of the earrings between her finger and thumb.

'Is this just a dream?' Karen asked. 'Please tell me it isn't Kelly,' she added and started to sniffle. 'No, it's not a dream, honest,' Kelly said, and she sat on the bed and she hugged her sister hard. She felt real – she was no ghost. Kelly suddenly removed one of her earrings and put it in her sister's palm and then she closed that palm for her and said, 'Take this Karen, just so you'll know you never dreamt all this.'

'No, it's yours,' Karen tried to hand the earring back but Kelly shook her head and clasped her sister's hand and closed it again. She then stood up, and said: 'I have to go now, Karen, but I'll always be looking over you. Bye Karen.'

Karen woke up in tears, and she looked in her hand, and there was nothing there. She looked in the other hand and saw nothing – no earring. And then she saw the golden earring on the duvet, and there was no doubt about it – it was one of the earrings she had bought for her sister. Those earrings were left on her sister's earlobes and Karen had personally watched them place the lid on her sister's coffin and she knew no one had removed them. Karen showed the earring to her husband and he went to the jewellers – H. Samuel – where the earrings had been purchased and an expert in the store confirmed that it was one of the earrings Karen had purchased. Karen's husband could still not accept that his sister-in-law had returned from the grave to give her sister a little tangible memento of her visit, but to this day, Karen believes Kelly did come back from beyond that Boxing Day to comfort her big sister, and she carries that earring everywhere she goes on a chain around her neck.

Tom Slemen

HAG NIGHT

There is no legal reason which prohibits the marriage of a couple on Christmas Day, although of course, that day is one of the busiest dates of the year in the Church, but many people are on such close terms with their priests and vicars, they often arrange to have the wedding service between the other services on the day. In Victorian times, Christmas Day marriages were quite common for several reasons; marriage on Christmas Day and Christmas Eve was seen as a more romantic way of tying the knot, but in times past, marriages on December 25th (and also on Easter Sunday) were free – the Church never charged for the service, and sometimes up to half a dozen couples would be married at once at Christmas. Of course, marriage in the Victorian period was a lot less complicated and less expensive than it is now; the banns of marriage would be read for just three consecutive Sundays and the couple could just turn up at the church without any rehearsal – and that was it. Today, it's a different matter of course, and weddings can be astronomically expensive. In Liverpool, in 2003, a couple in their early twenties named Tamlyn and Matt had decided to walk up the aisle on Christmas

Day at a fairly well-known church on Merseyside, and of course, the Saturday before the marriage, which fell on 20th December, was Matt's Stag night. Matt wanted a quiet Stag night with only four friends, and these four mates of his said that was fair enough, but when Saturday came, eighteen of his friends, including several cousins he didn't even get on with, arrived in a minibus at his house in West Derby and took him on the town. Matt worked in the catering business and was a part-time Territorial Army soldier, and a rather level-headed lad, but he knew from past experience that once he got past five pints of lager, he would become quite aggressive and would also want to go from club to club till the sun was coming up. His friends plied him with lager, wine, shorts, all types of shots and even absinthe – and at one point, Matt was held down as one of his cousins produced an electric cordless razor and shaved his head. By four o'clock it was snowing heavily in the city centre, and the police had moved on the Stag party gang from Mathew Street. The revellers then split up into two groups after fighting with one another over an argument concerning football. Matt had been dressed in a Santa outfit by now and was so drunk he could hardly speak, and kept asking to be taken home to his beloved Tamlyn. Matt's closest friend, Sean, stuffed a box containing a 24-inch-pizza into his hands and told him to shut up. At this point, a stray dog which looked part Alsatian, began to follow the lads, and they nicknamed the dog Deano for some reason. Matt fed the pizza to Deano and the dog followed him and the gang to a bus stop, where they all sat hurtling insults at passers by. 'Take me home to Tamlyn,' Matt pleaded, 'she'll be worried sick about me. Take me home, please fellahs,' and Matt hugged a whining Deano, but his friends just laughed, for they had other plans, and they carried him to Maryland Street, a little narrow street just off Rodney Street, one of the oldest thoroughfares in Liverpool with rows of terraced Georgian houses. Matt was tied to a 20 mph speed-limit post with a heavy rope by a towering muscular mate nicknamed Kevvo, and when Matt asked to be freed in a slurred voice, he was pelted with snowballs. His so-called mates and a few of his cousins then left the scene laughing and shouting.

Matt tried to get up but when he did the street seemed to swing about and he felt sick. He swore and cursed Kevvo and the others, and kept muttering to himself about going home to Tamlyn. He shouted for help, but a strange silence fell, along with the snow, and he tried to undo the knots of the rope tied around his neck, waist and leg, but his fingers were frozen and so he slipped about as he tried to get up. Not a car passed by on this Sunday morning, and Matt began to seriously worry about dying of hypothermia, because under the Santa outfit he was naked. His friends had thrown all of his clothes and underwear in a bin somewhere in town. The only things they'd left on him were his expensive ankle boots.

Matt heard something. It sounded like a voice. He looked to his right, but saw only the old red-brick wall of a cemetery there. This was adjacent to St Andrew's Church, which had lain derelict since the 1970s. Like most Liverpudlians, Matt knew about the huge black pyramid-shaped tomb in the cemetery behind that wall which was said to contain the body of a Victorian gambler who had been sealed up with a winning hand of poker cards in his stiff hands after death. The man had lost his soul in a poker game with the Devil himself, according to the old legend, and because Satan had promised to drag the defeated gambler down into the bowels of Hell as soon as he was laid in the earth, the canny card-player had been entombed *above* ground to avoid eternal damnation. The earthbound ghost of the Victorian in the pyramidal tomb had been seen by countless people in Liverpool over the years, and they say he walks because he can't go to Hell and Heaven won't have him because he had burnt a Bible as a young man when his sweetheart had died from a fever. So was the voice which Matt had just heard the mutterings of the ghostly Devil-dodger?

There it was again. And this time it sounded like the voice of an old woman, and what shocked the intoxicated Matt was the fact that this woman, who was still out of sight, was using some very coarse and obscene language. Then she came around the corner from the opposite direction he had expected her to come from – from the left - because her cussing had echoed off the cemetery wall to his right.

He lifted himself up slightly and the world began to sway as if he was on a ship in a storm. Then he saw her – or should I say, *it*?

People talk about being sobered up by shocks, and most of the time they are talking through their backsides; it's all exaggeration, but when Matt set eyes upon this hideous, hunchbacked thing waddling towards him, he felt his heart pound like a pneumatic hammer and he even forgot about the spinning street. It was something out of someone's darkest nightmare.

Matt still struggles to explain what he saw, and he has sketched the thing for me many times. It was what he could only describe as an old hag, but the face, which was heavily pock-marked, was barely human. It was very pale – almost white - with patches of red and purplish skin, and the nose was huge, wide as it was long, but curved, and above the bridge of the nose, thick bristly black eyebrows met in the middle of the forehead. The eyes of the monstrosity were dark and pink with almost luminous blue and silver irises and the bags below them were prominent bulging sacks of wrinkled skin. Long straight greyish silver hair fell from under the strange black hood the entity wore, and the huge mouth of the apparition was opening to show two rows of yellow and grossly misshapen teeth. Strands of grey saliva were dripping from this mouth, which was bordered with drooping red lips. The hag was bent over with a huge hump on her back, and as she walked along her abnormally long black pointed shoes protruded under the train of a black ragged robe. Matt swore as the thing approached and he tried desperately to undo the knots. The hands of the hag looked freakishly long with elongated fingers and they reached out towards the terrified young man. 'I'll have you, you f___g c___,' she rasped, and Matt screamed for help as he tried to undo the huge knot which tethered him to the post, but it was tied too hard. Matt therefore grabbed the grey metal post and tried to rock it back and forth, attempting to uproot it from the pavement. The paving flag at the base of the post did budge slightly but it was no use – that pole was anchored by a huge chunk of concrete beneath that flag.

He slipped and landed on his backside and swore with nerves.

She was upon him now, and she tried to grab his left leg by the ankle, but he kicked his feet about in a frenzy and the heel of his left boot was thrust hard into the hag's face.

It felt as if he was kicking a ball of dough with a skull inside.

She cried out, and then spat at him and gritted her ghastly yellow teeth as blood dripped with the saliva from the top of her squirming mouth. She looked stunned, shocked at him doing that, and all of a sudden her mouth opened twice as wide, and she let out a deafening shriek – and charged at Matt with a strange shuffling motion. He could hardly breathe as she pinned him down, and she slapped him with both of her ice-cold bony long-fingered hands, and he saw her bloodied saliva drip into his left eye as he cried out. He distinctly heard one of his ribs crack and two bulbous wrinkled objects pressed down on his abdomen under her black robe, and as he thrashed about with his fists at the thing's face, she made rhythmic up-and-down movements, as if she was trying to have sex with him. Her black garment, which had a horrible stench about it, moved aside as he lashed out, and he could see that the two bulbed objects pressing down on his abdomen were the hag's breasts, and they had hairy nipples and were covered with melanomas and warts.

'Get off me you bastard! Get off me! Get off me!' Matt screamed, and he panicked because he could not draw in his breath. And then he saw a figure to his right! Someone had turned up after hearing his cries, and he saw that it was a man of around his own age in jeans and a dark blue long-sleeved shirt.

'Help me mate!' Matt tried to shout but he had no air left in his lungs now.

The man he had spotted didn't even turn around, but unzipped and urinated against the cemetery wall, and he stood there with his head craned back in relief.

The hag stopped and looked over her shoulder at the young man, then turned back to look at the asphyxiated Matt. 'He can't see me,' she cackled, 'no one can see me, just you lovey.'

'Help.' Matt's attempt to cry was just a whisper, and he felt as if he was about to die. In his mind he suddenly pictured the Sacred Heart. This image came from the depths of his memory – from the days of his childhood. When he was seven, his Nan had given him a beautiful gold-leaf Bible with that image of Jesus, gazing with sorrowful eyes up into heaven, on the cover of the book. How strange, that this image had surfaced now when Matt felt as if he was facing death.

There was a loud growl!

The hag screamed and started to shake; no, something was shaking her! It was that dog Matt had befriended earlier – Deano. The part-Alsatian dog bit through the black robe into the flesh of the hag's crooked back, and blood sprayed onto the snow. Matt smiled faintly as the hag lifted herself off him and clawed at the dog, and at one point the animal seized the unearthly being's twig-like fingers and ripped two of them off.

From the other side of the narrow street, the man who had been relieving himself zipped up and shouted, 'Hey lad, is that your dog?'

Matt was of course, unable to answer with a lung pierced by the sharp edge of a cracked rib. He nodded and thought, 'What an idiot. Can't he see the state I'm in? Why doesn't he call an ambulance?'

'You wanna keep it under control lad or you'll get done,' the young man advised. He then came slowly across the road, keeping an eye on Deano – who looked as if he was fighting with his own shadow, because the hag was not visible to the stranger.

Matt lifted his arm and reached to the stranger in a gesture for help.

'Who tied you to the post, lad?' he asked, and at this point, Matt blacked out. He woke up in the Royal Teaching Hospital sometime later, and he tried to tell a nurse what had happened, and then he felt a soft hand in his, and he realised that Tamlyn was at his bedside, and her eyes were red raw from crying. He tried to tell her what had happened but in a broken, choked-up voice she told him not to speak. He had been minutes from death after a broken rib punctured his lung and air had started to fill his chest. A local medical student living on Rodney Street had saved Matt's life by plunging a needle into his side, releasing the air that had escaped from his lung only to be trapped between the lung and the chest wall. The build-up of escaped air which accumulates from the lung stops it from expanding as fully as it normally does, and this condition is called pneumothorax. The doctors assumed the cracked rib had been caused by a drunken Matt having a bad fall in the snow.

When Matt eventually recovered he told Tamlyn about the old hag, and she assured him that it had all been some hallucination brought on by all of the drinking – especially the shots of absinthe, which was notorious for inducing weird visions. Matt said he was 100% sure the thing had been real, and when he claimed that it had tried to have its way with him, Tamlyn smiled and shook her head, and said that perhaps someone had spiked one of his drinks that night. The couple had to postpone their Christmas marriage and wed on a new date in January. By then, there was another guests at the wedding – Deano. Matt and Tamlyn had walked the streets around Chinatown, where Matt had vague recollections of first setting eyes upon the dog, and they had found him roaming around Duke Street. Matt believes to this day that the dog saved his life from something evil he cannot explain. Perhaps the hag was a thing called a succubus - a demonic ghastly-looking woman who tries to have intercourse with men in their beds – especially men who are run-down health-wise – or heavily intoxicated or drugged. The annals of the occult are rife with reports of these nocturnal assaults. In modern times, psychologists have noted an increase in the aptly-named Old Hag Syndrome; this is a condition where a person awakes in bed and discovers that he or she cannot move a muscle – and they usually feel something heavy on their chest. Some have reported seeing an ugly old woman sitting on their chest, preventing them from breathing as they lie there stricken with paralysis. I have investigated many of these cases and noted how they are almost always reported in clusters, sometimes with the "old hag" preying on people who live in the same street. Whilst most psychologists believe the old hag is merely a figment of a person suffering from a sleep-paralysis disorder coupled with disrupted rapid-eye movement, I would beg to differ, for I have noticed how professional and rational observers such as doctors and policemen have also described the old hag as she 'rides' them by sitting heavily on their chests. The descriptions of the hag's stomach-churning odour, her horrible discoloured teeth, and often, her hairy tongue (which she sometimes slides into the mouth of the victim) seem rather too consistent to be mere hallucinations, and it makes me wonder if people living alone who have supposedly died of heart failure or 'natural causes' in their beds were in fact victims of the demonic old hag…

THE MISSING ROOM

One grey wintry afternoon in the 1930s, a 47-year-old cleaner named Joan was mopping the floor of a certain well-known Catholic church in Leicestershire, and on this day she really had her work cut out because her workmate Elsie was off with a bad dose of the flu, so, on her own, poor Joan had to mop the entire floor of the church – the nave, transept, and the aisles. She halted near a confession box, looked about, and satisfied that the church was empty, she lit a cigarette and sat on a bench. She heard a deep sonorous voice, and it was emanating from the confessional. Joan was a very nosy person, and she just couldn't help herself, and so he looked around again, and then she sneaked in her flat shoes to the heavy oaken door of the booth and listened. Her mouth formed a letter O when she heard the shocking details of the confessor. He said, 'I have been very weak and I succumbed to the temptations of the flesh…'

Joan took a quiet drag on her Woodbine and exhaled through her nose as she listened to the rest of the scandalous revelations from the well-spoken penitent. The confession went on for almost twenty-five minutes, and then, as the priest was giving absolution, Joan picked up her mop and bucket and darted away to the opposite side of the church. She got the shock of her life when she saw who the penitent was. A bishop came out of that confession box holding a floppy black fedora, and he kept his head bowed as he walked down the aisle towards the church door.

'Bloody Hell,' Joan whispered, then realising what she had said she turned to face the crucifix above the altar and quickly made the sign of the cross saying, 'Oh, sorry.'

She watched the bishop leave and thought about the very strange tale he had told as he had confessed his sins. Joan told her flu-stricken friend Elsie every single sordid detail about the rambling story she had heard, and Elsie in turn told someone else, and what you are about to read is the very tale nosy Joan heard that day outside the door of the confession booth.

In December 1932, a certain bishop in his late sixties was giving a service at a cathedral, when a beautiful young lady caught his eye among the congregation. He had never seen her before but was taken aback by her pretty face and beautiful, shapely figure. Days after the service he was visiting a colleague at the archdiocese building in the town one snowy afternoon when he again set eyes on the attractive woman as she waited at a tram stop. The bishop suddenly slipped in the slush and fell on his back. The beauty saw him fall and came running to his aid. She knelt by him and thrust out a gloved hand which he grasped as he looked into her huge green eyes, and now, at closer quarters as she helped him up, he could see she was even lovelier than he had thought, and in a silky voice she asked if he was alright.

'Oh, yes, thankyou. How silly of me to slip,' said the Bishop.

She brushed the snow from his back and then giggled as she wiped the slush and granulated ice from his backside, and the senior member of the clergy felt a pleasurable electric sensation course through his body, and he felt such guilt afterwards.

'Thankyou miss – ' the Bishop said, red-faced with embarrassment.

'Meer,' said the lady, 'Lucy Meer.'

'Thankyou Lucy,' the Bishop said, and he wanted to say he had seen her during the church service but resisted because he felt it would lead to something inappropriate.

'Oh, here's my tram!' Lucy exclaimed and she dashed off to the tram stop as she shouted: 'Bye bye!'

That night the Bishop had very erotic dreams about Lucy in which she was lying naked next to him on a large bed in a spacious white room with sunlight bursting through the net curtains. He was nude too, and she was caressing his chest and her hand was resting on his pot belly.

He awoke with a start to the sound of the bedside alarm clock, and he pondered upon the dream for a while. He felt so venal. Was someone – something metaphysical – perhaps Him - subjecting him to temptations of a carnal nature, perhaps as a test? Or after a lifetime of sexual repression was he simply over-reacting to perfectly natural feelings and emotions most men had in the company of beautiful women? But she was so young – barely into her twenties by the looks of her - and he was so old in comparison, but he suddenly heard a rather coarse part of his psyche say from the back of his mind: 'The bee always pollinates the freshest flower.'

Two days later the Bishop had to travel to Liverpool to attend an important meeting, the last one of the year, with several other church officials, and who should he find himself sharing his compartment with on the train but Miss Meer. He tilted his hat at the lady as she sat opposite him, and she said hello and then politely enquired about his destination.

'Liverpool,' the Bishop told her, and looked at the other two passengers – two elderly women – seated in the compartment.

'Same here!' Lucy announced with a beaming smile of milk white teeth and lips of scarlet. She wore a royal blue petal-trimmed cloche hat and a C-shaped curl was protruding over the right side of her forehead, above a thin, perfectly arched eyebrow. She wore a polka-sot scarf around her neck and a dark tweed into-the-waist jacket. Her long shapely legs were crossed and the Bishop could see their contoured outlines pressed against the long grey calf-length skirt. Her narrow black patent leather shoe pointed its toe towards him and that shoe see-sawed as she asked: 'Are you going to see relatives too?'

The Bishop did not want the two old dears in the compartment to know who he was – just in case he *did* decide to take things further, so he did not dare mention his Episcopal position and identify himself. And so he said: 'Going to see some friends, actually.'

The Bishop and Lucy conversed as if they had known one another for years throughout the first leg of the journey – to Birmingham's New Street, where they had to change trains. The Bishop took the young lady to the station café where they shared a pot of tea and Lucy enjoyed a delicious slice of sandwich cake at the Bishop's expense. By the time they had reached Liverpool's Lime Street Station, the Bishop had been wholly seduced by Lucy, and she had her stockinged foot in his crutch as the train was pulling in, and the blissful Bishop had his eyes closed as the train jolted to a halt. Lucy withdrew her leg and remained seated opposite. She was putting her shoe back on when the guard came into the compartment. Thinking the Bishop was asleep the guard shouted, 'Lime Street, Liverpool!'

Lucy took a handkerchief out of her handbag and wiped the traces of her lipstick from the Bishop's mouth.

'The guard didn't see that on my mouth, did he?' the Bishop asked, full of concern.

'No, he didn't you silly worry-wart,' she reassured him.

The Bishop decided it would be the Imperial Hotel, and not the Adelphi, where he could possibly be recognised by the staff and administration, as he had attended a church charity ball there last Christmas. The Imperial was a much inferior three-star hotel and he had never visited the place before, but had often seen it whenever he was visiting the city because it was facing Lime Street Station.

They booked in as a married couple under the predictable surname of Jones, and the Bishop felt as if he was in a dream. They sat on the bed, and Lucy began to kiss him, and he pulled away.

'What's the matter?' she asked, unbuttoning her blouse.

'Nothing, I'm just a little nervous,' the Bishop said, and he stood up and looked out of the window at a snow-covered Lime Street. Some of the shops had coloured lights in their windows and a man was selling pine Christmas trees from his handcart. Down on St

George's Plateau a Salvation Army brass band was playing some vaguely familiar tune, probably a carol.

'Come on, come to bed,' said Lucy, pulling back the sheets of the old iron framed bed. She was only in her brassiere and drawers now.

The Bishop turned from the window and seemed so stunned at the sight of the scantily-clad lady. His mouth opened as if he was about to speak but no words came forth, and his face blushed.

'What's wrong?' Lucy asked, taking off the brassiere. 'Don't you like my birthday suit?'

'You know what I find so strange about you, Lucy?' the Bishop suddenly said, and he thinned his eyes and cast a suspicious glance at her.

'What do you mean?' she asked, getting into the bed.

He remained in front of the window. 'You never asked me what my first name is, and that's quite strange, but I was blinded by your beauty. I was under your spell.'

'Well, what *is* your name?' Lucy asked with a childish grin, and she sat in the bed, bare-breasted and tapped the vacant pillow to her right.

'I'm a bishop, and I have a feeling you already know that.'

'I don't understand,' Lucy said, 'Come to bed and explain.'

'Lucy, I have the charism, do you know what that is?' the Bishop said, and now the blush had gone from his face and he walked towards his suitcase.

'No, I don't, and I don't know what you're talking about at all,' she told him, and seemed ready to burst into tears by the look on her porcelain face.

'Charism is the power to do good that flows from

God,' the Bishop said, and then he paused as he heard the strains of *O Come All Ye Faithful* from the Salvation Army band. 'And I have obtained Charism from God through an unbroken chain of bishops stretching back to St Peter. An unbroken chain from God, by the laying on of hands over centuries from bishop to bishop.'

As he said this latter sentence, Lucy *changed* into something that looked like a cross between a reptile and a segmented black insect, and although the instant transformation scared the Bishop, he calmly walked to his suitcase, took out the Bible and a crucifix on a chain. He put the chain around his neck and held out the Bible at the scaled and horned entity with the twisted grin. It made farting noises with its mouth and some sort of short black bristly tail between its legs began to flip from side to side like the tail of a thwarted cat.

The Bishop put on his coat and hat, and then he backed away towards the door, only to find there was no door - just dingy flocked wallpaper.

In Latin, the grotesque thing on the bed told him he was damned and had no faith, even though he was supposed to be a modern-day Apostle.

The Bishop looked desperately for the door, but it simply wasn't there.

And suddenly an alarm bell began to ring, and it never stopped. It was a fire alarm, and the sounds of raised voices and running feet could be heard. Unknown to the Bishop, at this time, the manager ran up to the second floor, where the Bishop was, but could not find room 12A. There was no Room 13 at the Imperial, and there is no Room 13 at most hotels for superstitious reasons, so most hotels who omit that room number designate it 12A instead. But the manager and assistant manager could not find the door to Room 12A. It was as if the room had vanished. They could see the stretch of wall where the door should have been, and they even rapped their knuckles on the wall there and cried to "Mr and Mrs Jones" but received no reply. The manager and his assistant were then forced to flee the building as thick smoke from a fire in the basement reached the second floor corridor.

'Let me out of here in the name of the Lord and his Son Jesus Christ!' the Bishop shouted at the demon, who remained seated in the bed. It imitated the breaking wind sound in a childish manner again and cackled before spouting Latin insults.

The Bishop could smell the acrid smoke now, and suddenly he saw that the door had reappeared in the wall behind him and the poisonous vapour was coming through the half-inch gap under the door. The Bishop raised the Bible above his head, ready to toss it at the insectoid creature – but the thing had vanished. The Bishop opened the door and walked into blinding, choking grey clouds, and somehow, despite stumbling and falling down a flight of stairs, he made it into the foyer, where daylight was filtering through from the street. He staggered outside into the arms of the Salvation Army bandleader and lost consciousness. He was taken to the Liverpool Infirmary and treated for smoke inhalation, and was discharged within the week. He never set eyes upon "Lucy Meer" again nor did he ever learn who she was, and he never expected to, because the Bishop knew that the young lady had been a subtle illusion of something from that infernal region where evil people go after death – the place, where, as the Bible says, they 'walk the darkness'. I researched this eerie case and discovered that that same year, in the same month, on the morning of Christmas Eve, a blaze broke out at Summergreene's Golden Fleece Hotel at Liverpool – but it was the Liverpool in Sydney, Australia – and at this fire, a very strange incident took place. A room occupied by a couple who were supposedly married could not be found as the manager went around the premises in an attempt to evacuate the building. On this occasion, the couple were forced to climb out of the window because they had been unable to find the door in their room, and spoke of seeing strange shadows on the walls and of hearing weird voices. The couple concerned were married – but not to each other – and believed the disappearance of the door in their room had been the work of the Devil. The manager said the couple had just been disoriented by the smoke, as the door was still there, but the couple stopped seeing one another and returned to their spouses.

THE CHRISTMAS GHOST SHIP

From my many years of investigating the unknown I have come to realise that there are many worlds – not just the billions of distant unexplored but statistically inhabited planets beyond this solar system – but the worlds which exist 'beside' our one like the parallel pages of a book. Some of the beings which inhabit these other realms occasionally come into our world either by accident or choice – that is my belief, and more and more scientists who are gradually unravelling the complex topsy-turvy rules of quantum physics are beginning to say the same; they believe we live not in a *uni*verse but a *multi*verse of countless parallel worlds – infinite variations of the universe which exist side by side.

Sometimes, when the beings from these worlds 'next door' come into our one, they are interpreted as Little Green Men from a flying saucer, demons from Hell, angels from heavenly realms, the Abominable Snowman, Bigfoot, fairies and so on; it all depends on the culture and mindset of the people who encounter these beings from other dimensions. For example, there is a report in *The Times* of London for June 5, 1908, which touches on a very bizarre incident which took place at Port Dinorwic – now known as Y Felinheli – a village beside the Menai Straits in North Wales. The report states that on Sunday 31 May, 1908, a Mrs Roberts, the middle-aged wife of a quarryman in Port Dinorwic, became ill, and vomited up two very strange creatures which resembled tiny naked men about three inches in length. She had felt these creatures 'crawling up her gullet' just before she felt the intense urge to vomit. The woman said the creatures looked like prawns in colour and shape, and another report in another newspaper states that these miniature beings were alive when she vomited them up, but they later died and turned black on one side and retained a delicate pink colour on the other. The unidentified creatures were taken away by the family doctor, a Mr Edwards, and being unable to ascertain what the things were, he passed them on to a Dr Cunnington, Acting Professor of Zoology at Bangor University College, but even his expert eyes failed to identify the species the creatures belonged to, nor could he explain how they got into the stomach of Mrs Roberts. Other newspapers published differing reports of this weird incident, with one article stating that the little beings had lived in the woman's stomach for two years. The only theory Cunnington could advance was that perhaps Mrs Roberts had somehow swallowed the ovum or germ of the creatures via the drinking water. The final word on the unknown creatures – from another "expert" – was that they were some sort of crayfish. This case reminds me of a very similar occurrence which is alleged to have taken place at Dublin in the 1970s. A woman in her twenties named O'Hare became ill one morning and went to the toilet to be sick. She knelt before the toilet bowl and vomited something up. She was then astounded to see a tiny naked man, about two inches in length, thrashing about in the water bowl. Mrs O'Hare ran to tell her husband what had happened and he refused to get out of bed at first and said she was seeing things. He eventually went into the toilet and saw that his wife had been telling the truth, and that a tiny human-like figure with a little mop of black hair was trying to climb up the ceramic wall of the toilet bowl. Mrs O'Hare had red hair and Mr O'Hare had sandy blonde hair, and he mentioned this fact then suddenly accused his wife of having an affair and said that the thing in the toilet bowl with the black hair was some sort of miscarried baby! As Mrs O'Hare recoiled in shock at the ridiculous accusation, Mr O'Hare began to swear, and he flushed the toilet – but the little man was still there, and the couple could hear a faint high-pitched sound coming from the miniscule naked man – as if he was crying for help. Mr O'Hare then grabbed the toilet brush from its holder and began holding the miniature humanoid under the water. His wife screamed for him to stop and he took her concern for some sort of maternal feeling towards the unearthly Lilliputian and tried to flush the toilet again but the cistern hadn't yet filled up. Less than a minute later Mr O'Hare managed to flush the toilet again and this time the little man was successfully flushed away, and Mr O'Hare also emptied bleach into the toilet bowl as a precaution. There is no known way a woman can miscarry a baby and vomit it up, and like the origin of the strange creatures Mrs Roberts threw up in 1908, the Dublin case remains a mystery. However, could it be possible that these little unknown humanoid creatures could be from another dimension where the scale of life is much reduced in comparison to the scale of our world? Five years after the Port Dinorwic case, in May 1913, at Farmersville, the "Onion Capital of North

Texas" which lies north-east of Dallas, something very strange – and still unexplained – took place one morning. Silbie Latham, a 12-year-old boy, and brothers Sid and Clyde, were chopping cotton on the family farm when their dogs – Fox and Bobby – began to bark and whine, and that usually meant a stranger was approaching. The Latham boys went to see what was upsetting the dogs and found the hounds about seventy-odd feet away on the other side of a picket fence. The three lads saw what the dogs were barking and growling at on the other side of that fence and they couldn't take it in at first. It was a small dark-green man about eighteen inches tall in a little sombrero type of hat. Like the little man Mrs O'Hare 'coughed up' and the humanoid Mrs Roberts disgorged, the little green man was naked. His green skin looked smooth but rubbery, and before the boys could get a closer look, their dogs tore the man to pieces and all that was left was a huge red blood stain on the ground and the remains of tiny human-like ruptured organs. The Latham children told their parents about the little green man but their strange account was not taken at all seriously, even though those three kids had been very honest and God-fearing because of their strict upbringing. The next day a few curious adults went to the spot were the supposed little man had been killed by the dog, but there wasn't even a trace of blood or any remains whatsoever. Today, the story is usually interpreted in our Space Age culture as possible evidence of a visitation by an extraterrestrial being, but the little man in the wide-brimmed hat could equally be interpreted as a visitor from a neighbouring dimension who came into our one intentionally or through some poorly understood force of nature which brought him here. Could such a force be responsible for the many perplexing disappearances of people, animals, planes, ships and other vehicles over the years? If such a force *can* sweep living beings and their machines into another dimension, could it have been responsible for the following Christmastime mystery?

On Friday, September 21 1928, a Danish five-masted barque named *Copenhagen*, employed as a naval cadet training vessel, left Nørresbundy in Northern Jutland and pointed her bows west as she headed for Buenos Aires under the command of seasoned and cautious master mariner Hans Andersen. A crew of 26 and 45 cadets were onboard the 430-foot-long *Copenhagen* and she presented a magnificent sight as she cut through the North Sea with her five masts (each more than 20 stories high) and her impressive figurehead of Bishop Absalon, the 12th century churchfather of Denmark and a prominent figure in the Danish campaigns to expand their territory. Down in the hold of the ship was a cargo of bagged cement and boxes of chalk. The sails on the five masts of the *Copenhagen* could take it around the world, and the collective area of their canvas was 56,000 feet, but the ship also had an auxiliary diesel engine, and it was also equipped with a modern wireless transceiver, although Captain Andersen was never one to use the transmitter unless it was a necessity. Although the *Copenhagen* was primarily used as a training ship for cadets, she offset most of her costs by carrying cargo during some of the voyages. As she left Nørresbundy she was making her tenth trip, and two of these trips had included the circumnavigation of the earth. The ship had virtually visited every continent since she first set out to sea in 1921. On Saturday 17 November 1928 she reached Buenos Aires and her cargo of cement and chalk was unloaded. The ship was then due to sail for Melbourne with another load of cargo from Buenos Aires but there were no paying commissions from any of the local firms to export anything to Australia, and so, on Friday 14 December, Captain Andersen sailed for Melbourne with an empty cargo hold on what should have been a 45-day journey. On 22 December the *Copenhagen* exchanged several radio messages with the *William Blumer* - a Norwegian steamship – and these communications established that "everything was well" and that the training barque's location was some 900 miles from Tristan da Cunha – the main island in a group of volcanic islands and one of the most remote places in the world. The plan was for the *Copenhagen* to dock at Melbourne, where a consignment of wheat would be picked up and brought back to Europe – but something strange happened which has never been explained. The radio operator of the *William Blumer* tried to contact the *Copenhagen* hours after the last exchange of messages, but there was no reply – merely the howls, clicks and hisses of atmospheric radio interference. More and more attempts were made to contact the Australia-bound vessel over Christmas, but the *Copenhagen* was never heard from again – but she was *seen* by many under very peculiar circumstances. The Danish East Asiatic Company, which had built the *Copenhagen* dispatched the *Mexico* - a fully modern motor vessel - to go and search for the missing ship around the waters of Tristan da Cunha but still no trace was found of the *Copenhagen* and the mystery only deepened when several islanders claimed that they had seen a gigantic five-masted ship with a broken foremast on 21 January 1929. This didn't make sense, because surely the Captain would have given orders to drop anchor and then he would have gone ashore until the mast was repaired. Instead the *Copenhagen* was seen to sail on until it was lost to sight on the horizon. The authorities doubted the claims of the islanders on Tristan da Cunha because at the time they supposedly saw the *Copenhagen* she would have been much further east. All the same the captain of the *Mexico* plotted the course the missing ship would have taken if she had indeed been the vessel seen by the islanders, and he ended up searching Gough Island, which lies just south of Tristan da Cunha, but he found no wreckage from the *Copenhagen* and no survivors from the absent ship. The Alfred Holt & Co Shipping line of Liverpool, England offered immediate assistance to the Danish authorities by diverting their steamer *Deucalion* after she had left Cape Town to search the Prince Edward islands, Crozet islands, as well as the Island of Kerguelan whilst on her way to Fremantle in Australia. The British Navy even helped in the search for the ship for months but in the end the Danish authorities decided that the *Copenhagen* had met with some disaster – possibly a night-time collision with an iceberg – and the Government of Denmark declared that the ship and all of its crew were now officially lost at sea. By now, the mysterious disappearance of the training ship was generating some strange rumours around the harbours and ports of the world. Sailors are a superstitious lot and the word on the maritime grapevine was that the disappearance of the *Copenhagen* had something to do with the occult, and of someone on board the vessel who was known to dabble with the Ouija board during voyages. The origins of these eerie rumours is unknown but they were rife in the maritime communities of the world.

The official announcement of the *Copenhagen* and her captain and crew being lost at sea was not the end of this mysterious matter, for over the years since the training ship vanished off the face of the earth, there have been many alleged sightings of the barque, and the first of these reports came in July 1930 when several members of the crew of an Argentinean freighter stated that they had seen a five-masted ship sailing along in a gale. The captain, a very superstitious man took statements from the crew members and opined that the ship they had seen was the 'wraith of the *Copenhagen*' sailing along like some latter-day *Flying Dutchman* because the souls of the long-dead crew were not at rest. More and more sightings of a huge ship with five masts were seen in the years following these early reports, including a very sinister one in December 1949. A young able-bodied seaman from Liverpool named John Jones worked on a ship called the *Columbia* (formerly the *Katoomba*) and in November 1949 it left Genoa, bound for Fremantle, Australia on 17 December. Jones was to stay on the ship after that date to dock at Sydney on Boxing Day, where he was due to join a party of friends for a Christmas celebration at a tavern. When the Columbia was about 800 miles to the south-east of Madagascar's southern coast, John Jones went on deck to smoke his pipe. To the stern of the ship, the sun was setting and so twilight was falling, and there were only three other people on the deck. One of these other people was an Irish passenger who was playing Christmas carols on a guitar, and Jones took a few puffs on his pipe and started to sing along when the guitarist played the old English carol *I Saw Three Ships*. then the most extraordinary thing took place which haunted John Jones till they day he died in the 1980s. Jones sang the line: 'I saw three ships come sailing in, on Christmas Day, on Christmas day...'

Then the guitarist stopped playing and looked past the Liverpudlian. Jones followed his gaze, and turning around he saw something which was unfamiliar and terrifying at first. Silhouetted against the blood-orange clouds upon which the setting sun was shining, there was a long black object that looked like a cigar at arms length, but the rightmost end of the object resembled the head of a dolphin – or perhaps a swordfish, because the 'nose' projected to a sharp point. The other end of this fuselage-shaped body – the end furthest away - tapered to a gental curving slope like the blade of a knife. From this weird airborne horizontal black beam there hung five long 'legs' with smaller beams at right angles to them...

'Jesus Christ!' Jones cried out, realising that the thing sailing silently and slowly towards the *Columbia* through the air was an upside-down ship. The Irishman dropped the guitar and fled across the deck, ready to jump over the rail, fearing, as Jones did, a catastrophic collision. The mind of John Jones could not take in what he was seeing, because it was such a surreal sight. How on earth could a ship be turned upside down so that its masts are dangling downwards, almost touching the sea, and its hull and rudder are facing the sky? What titanic force could possibly keep a massive vessel of such great tonnage aloft? The ship suspended in the air seemed to b about 500 feet from nose to stern, and Jones estimate the tonnage as being about four thousand tons – about half the tonnage of the ship he was travelling on. Those inverted masts would cut through the hull of the *Columbia* and open her like a tin of sardines. The two other men on deck were Italian shiphands and they cried something in their native tongue and ran to the stern of the ship in a futile attempt to escape what would surely be the most unearthly sea disaster of all time. John Jones stood rooted to the spot, paralysed with fear, transfixed with what he saw as his nemesis – but within a few seconds the shadowy upturned ship passed by, sailing overhead at about thirty knots or more, and the ends of the masts seemed like thirty feet away as they passed by. The *Columbia* sailed on, and it transpired that no lookouts had seen the weird spectacle, just John Jones, the Irishman and the two Italians, and one of the Italian men spoke excitedly in broken English to his countryman, and Jones could make out the word '*Copenhagen*'. The Irishman squinted at the sunset and exclaimed, 'Oh my! Look at that!'

As the sun went down into the sea, there was a small flash of green light just before it was obscured fully by the horizon. This is a poorly understood meteorological effect that has been observed by mariners for centuries. As the green flash of light emanated from the tip of the setting sun, the unmanned upside-down sailing ship could be briefly seen contrasted against the momentary glare as a stark shadow. And then nothing. The derelict in the sky had vanished. The *Columbia* duly arrived at Fremantle, and then on the next day it set sail for Sydney, berthing there on Boxing Day. John Jones told his friends what he had seen as they drank in a tavern near to the harbour, and an old Australian man told the Scouser that he had seen a vision of the *Copenhagen* which had vanished without a trace twenty-one years before. Was the upturned ship some ghostly apparition, or was it the solid ship itself? What could levitate a ship like that, and what happened to the 75 souls who had been on the vessel over two decades before when it vanished into Limbo? Was there any truth in the rumours about the Ouija board session on the *Copenhagen*? So many questions, and they'll probably never be answered; the sea keeps her secrets well.

A CHRISTMAS EXORCISM

In December 1983, a couple living together named Harriet and Neville – both in their twenties – decided to have a Christmas dinner for their friends: two couples - Clive and Cynthia and Hannah and Glynn – and the certified cynical singleton Trevor - who Neville had known since infant school. The dinner would be held at Harriet and Neville's little cottage, which lay in the green hills of south Somerset, not far from Cadbury Castle, the fabled site of Camelot. The cottage had been left to Harriet – a rather dreamy and impractical girl who was originally from Liverpool – by her eccentric Aunt Prudence when she was just eighteen – and the dwelling, a wattle and daub affair - dated back to Tudor times. It was all low ceilings with oak beams and the walls were nothing but interwoven rods and twigs covered in clay – all topped with a thatched roof. Neville thought the cottage was structurally unsound and was convinced a gale force would finish the place off one day. When Harriet first moved into the place it had no electricity or gas, and the décor and furniture had been that antique, it seemed as if Shakespeare had just popped out for an inspirational stroll on Windwhistle Hill and would be back any minute to finish his play. In 1980 the cottage was finally connected to the National Grid and the gas was plumbed in later. Neville was a nesh soul and had pleaded to have double-glazing put in for two years now but Harriet preferred the old Elizabethan style windows, even though they were draughty. At least the couple had an open fire for Christmas, something Harriet had always appreciated at this time of year, and she had run lengths of silver and gold tinsel across the stone mantelpiece and had decorated the old brass carriage clock on it with the obligatory holly and ivy – even though Neville said it added a 'general tackiness' to the place. A real pine Christmas tree stood in the corner festooned with multicoloured fairy lights and more tinsel but Neville had sawn off almost two feet of the tree because of the low ceiling in the living room.

From the big old black cast-iron hob in the kitchen came an aroma of roast beef, and there Harriet was at work. She had sprouts, carrots and peas on the boil, potatoes roasting in the oven above the huge joint of silverside beef, which she continually basted. Neville's annual jobs were to make the gravy and help lay the table. He had overdone it a bit this year with the addition of another smaller table upon which he would place plates of warm mince pies, a Christmas cake and sherry trifle his mum had made, an oversized Christmas pudding Harriet's friend Hannah had made, bowls of the usual nuts, and stollen, which was solely for Trevor, his old mate. And there were the usual crackers placed on both tables with the flimsy scarlet, yellow and green paper party hats and pathetic jokes.

At the feet of Harriet, her ginger tabby, Marmalade sat, sniffing the myriad aromas and forever getting under her feet. Every now and then he would gaze at the door with wide eyes and freeze – and Harriet would say, 'Is this them now?' – thinking Marmalade could hear the approach of the guests, but God knows what was attracting the cat's attention, because Harriet would see no one through the window on the path outside.

Neville had the wine bottles lined up. Cheap Concorde for Trevor, two expensive bottles of Beaujolais Nouveau for Clive and Cynthia, nothing but R. White's lemonade for Hannah and Glynn as they didn't drink – even at Christmas, and Hannah had also quit smoking because she was two months' pregnant. That reminded Neville; he'd bought a packet of Falstaff cigars for Trevor, but where had he put them?

Marmalade cried and hissed as he looked through the doorway of the kitchen towards the front door across the hallway.

'That's got to be Trevor arriving,' Harriet deduced. Marmalade hated Trevor and always hissed at him.

Neville opened the front door, looked down the path, and saw no one. He went as far as the wooden gate and raised himself on his toes to peer over the hedge. No, no one about. That stupid cat.

He came back and told Harriet no one was there and she noticed that Neville hadn't closed the door properly.

'Nev, close the door before he gets out,' she said, looking down at Marmalade, who was now arched into a horseshoe shape as he gazed at the gap in the front door. There was a she-cat in heat knocking about and just a month ago such a cat seduced Marmalade with her scent and he followed her for about ten miles and got lost for four days.

'Alright, alright!' Neville went back across the hallway and as he closed the door he heard the gate outside squeak. He opened the door again and saw two men – one had a black bob of hair to his shoulders and a black moustache, and reminded Neville of Trevor Eve, the actor who played the detective in that series *Shoestring* on the telly. A tall thin man with short blonde hair shuffled up the path behind him.

'Excuse me, but er – ' the Shoestring lookalike said, and hesitated as if he was having difficulty trying to express himself as he panted from running.

'Whatever you're selling, we're not interested,' Neville told him grumpily and tried to close the door, but the visitor placed his well-polished brogue inside the doorway and prevented the door from closing.

'I'm not selling anything' sighed the stranger, wanly, fatigued. 'Look, you'll probably think I'm mad but I'm a psychic researcher and something very nasty has just sneaked into your house!'

'What?' Neville shot a condescending look at the man and made a grim attempt at a smile before kicking his shoe from the doorframe. 'Beat it!'

'Who is it?' Harriet shouted from the kitchen, and then she came into the hallway with a slotted spoon in her hand, but by then Neville had pushed the front door shut.

'Some nutter saying something nasty has just come into the cottage!' Neville told her, and then he looked through the frosted square window in the door and saw that the men were still standing there.

'What?' Harriet asked, and looked to the floor, thinking that perhaps a rat had run into the hallway. Neville saw her do this and said 'Nothing's come in here; it's just a gimmick! These two are probably con men.'

The letterbox opened and the eyes of the man with the moustache looked in, startling Harriet. 'We've been chasing this thing all the way from Windwhistle Hill – ' he was saying when Neville shouted and swore at him before threatening to call the police. The two men then reluctantly left.

'God! There are some con merchants about!' Neville fumed, and when he heard a rap behind him he turned and almost pulled the front door off its hinges. 'I'm warning you!' he yelled.

Clive and Cynthia stood there in shock.

'Oh, I'm sorry Cyn, sorry Clive – just chased two conmen from my door,' Neville explained, and looked between them towards the gate to see if the men were still there but they'd gone.

'I think we passed them just now,' said Clive, and Cynthia nodded.

'Come in, come in,' Neville told them, then asked: 'One of them look like Eddie Shoestring?'

'Yeah,' Cynthia said with a broad smile, and the other fellah looked like Robert Redford.'

'He didn't,' Clive shook his bald head as he stepped into the cottage before his wife. 'Looked nothing like him.'

'Said they were psychic investigators,' Neville told his friends as he closed the door after them.

Harriet hugged Cynthia and said she had lost weight and the two young women went into the kitchen to catch up on each other's lives, leaving Neville to try and chat with Clive – who talked about nothing but computers - a subject that did not interest Neville in the slightest. Thankfully, Trevor arrived a few minutes later, and then Hannah and Glynn called at the cottage, and Glynn immediately talked about football and Yeovil Town FC in particular.

The Christmas dinner went fairly well. Harriet and Neville and Cynthia and Clive gave a toast to Hannah and Glynn becoming parents.

'She hasn't had it yet,' said Trevor, rather insensitively, 'Talk about counting your chicks before they're hatched.'

Trevor always felt like the gooseberry at these types of get-togethers, and sneered when the couples held hands or kissed in front of him. 'God, I'm glad I'm out of all that,' he said, looking very uncomfortable, sprawled out on the sofa on his own, smoking a Falstaff cigar while the three couples each sat in a armchair with their partners perched on their knees.

Trevor droned on: 'At first they tell you they love you and they'll never leave you and then you live with them for a while and they show their true colours.'

'You talking about Pam, Trev?' Neville asked, innocently.

'No!' Trevor bawled, making Cynthia jump. 'I'm talking about the "fairer sex" in general; they're only good for one thing.'

'Oh, and what would that be, Trev?' Harriet asked.

Trevor got up, downed his half glass of Blue nun, shook his head, then said, 'Adiós!' and headed for the front door.

'Trevor, I wasn't having a go at you – ' Neville almost pushed Harriet off his knee trying to get out of the armchair.

Trevor ignored his half-hearted apology and turned

the door handle – but the door wouldn't budge.

'Trev – ' Neville rushed out of the room into the hallway.

'Unlock the door now,' Trevor snarled, 'I'm going.'

'Trevor I was not having a dig – '

'Open the door Neville before I break it down!' All of the rage was welling up in Trevor and he stepped aside so Neville could open the door for him.

Trevor fumbled with the lock and discovered that the door was jammed shut, and he told Trevor the door was stuck so Trevor pushed his friend aside and tried to open it. He couldn't. He therefore stormed through the hallway and went into the kitchen, and took the big key dangling from a hook. He inserted this key into the kitchen door which gave access to the back garden. But the key wouldn't turn.

'Let *me* try,' said Neville, meekly, so sorry he'd belittled Trevor in front of the other guests. Neville could not get the key to turn a millimetre.

'Oh, what a bleedin' house this is!' Trevor climbed over the sink and one of his big feet knocked over an ornamental glazed teapot shaped like a little house and it fell onto the draining board and smashed.

'What was that?' came Harriet's voice from the living room, along with a snigger from Glynn.

'I don't believe this!' Trevor turned the elongated S-shaped handle on the window but he couldn't yank it open. Only then did the two men in the kitchen realise something odd was going on.

'You smashed my teapot house!' Harriet said angrily, eyeing the spout and lid among the fragments on the draining board.

'I'll do more than that unless I get out of this

shithole!' Trevor cried, and realising he was defeated, he jumped down onto the kitchen floor and went back into the hallway to try the front door again. It was still impossible to open.

'Here, let me have a go!' Glynn gently pushed his pregnant wife Hannah aside, kissed her on the cheek and walked into the hallway.

'Oh, here we go, He-Man,' joked Hannah.

Glynn tried to turn the handle of the Yale lock, and found it would not budge. He checked if the latch was on. It wasn't. 'I think the lock's gone.' He tried it again. 'Yeah, definitely gone.'

'It's odd that the lock on the door to the back garden has gone as well, isn't it?' Neville said, as Trevor stood in a corner of the hallway, shaking his head as he looked at the wall.

'The window is definitely stuck as well,' said Harriet from the kitchen, trying to turn the handle on the window. Then she noticed something really strange. 'Nev, look at this.'

Neville came into the kitchen, followed by Glynn.

'It's just all black out there, like there's a thick fog or something,' Harriet told Neville, pointing at the strange scene beyond the kitchen window. Glynn peered out the window and said it was just a typical December fog.

Neville shook his head. 'You should be able to see the lamp post outside over on the right.'

From the living room came Clive's voice. 'It's the same in here, Harriet; you can't see a thing through the window.'

Harriet, Neville and Glynn hurried into the living room and looked out the window to see that Clive was right. It was as if someone had covered the windowpanes with thick black paint.

Harriet left the room and went upstairs. She looked out of the window and expected to see the distant lights of the village two miles away – but she could see nothing but blackness – and when she tried to open the window she discovered to her horror that the handle refused to turn. She hurried downstairs and told Neville about this.

'I *know* how to get out of here,' Trevor suddenly announced, and he went into the hallway and opened the little door under the stairs. It was the cubby hole where Neville stored the wood and coal. Trevor reached in and grabbed the axe Neville used to chop wood and split the big lumps of coal.

'Trev, don't start causing any damage with that – ' Neville backed away because his old friend looked demented.

Cynthia yelped and hugged Clive.

'What are you going to do with that?' Clive asked him.

'You'll see,' Trevor smirked as he went into the kitchen.

'Trevor! Don't start smashing that window! I'm warning you!' Harriet followed closely behind him.

'You must be a mind reader, Harriet,' Trevor laughed, and then turned and gritted his teeth. Through those teeth he hissed: 'Because that's what I'm gonna do.'

'Don't mate!' Neville advised him humbly.

Trevor swung his axe-wielding hand backwards, just missing Neville's head, then channelled all of his rage into smashing the kitchen window with that axe.

The axe went straight through one of the panes, and Trevor realised that the head of the axe had come off. He looked at the broken wooden shaft in his hand, then looked through the jagged hole in the windowpane. Outside there was *nothing* - just a black silent void, like interstellar space minus the stars and everything else.

'There's nothing there,' Trevor muttered, and he put his hand through the hole in the window. It was cold out there, but why was everything so black? Where was the garden below the window? Where had the path and the gate and lane gone? He started to panic but hid his fear as well as he could.

'You'll pay for that, you – you drunken vandal!' Harriet yelled, and she pushed Trevor aside and looked through the hole in the glass, and Neville did the same.

'It's just a thick fog, or some smog,' Clive said, and Cynthia seemed near to tears. She suffered from claustrophobia and began to take deep breaths. The idea of being unable to get out of the little cottage was pushing her towards a panic attack. It was like being trapped in a damaged submarine on the bed of the Atlantic to her. She started to tremble.

'Have a drink love,' Clive poured her a little glass of scotch. She refused it and started to hyperventilate.

Neville picked up the lid of the shattered ornamental teapot when Harriet wasn't looking and he carefully tossed it through the hole in the window – then listened. It should have smashed on the paving below the window, but there wasn't a sound. Glynn saw this experiment and he picked up a box of cooking matches, and struck one and threw it straight away through the hole in the windowpane, and he saw it fall well below the couple of feet between the window ledge and the ground. It was as if the house was suspended in some black all-enveloping void.

Trevor came into the kitchen and seemed to have been distracted from his sulking by the weird predicament. 'Just turned the telly on – just all dots and interference. Have a look.'

Neville and Glynn went into the living room and there was Cynthia laying on her back on the sofa, apparently choking as she tried to get enough air into her lungs, and to her right, the colour television was making a faint hissing noise as white noise came through the speakers and a blizzard of dots danced on the cathode ray tube.

Trevor went to the midi system and switched on the radio but was greeted with the same electronic hissing noise. He turned the huge metal dial and the orange indicator moved steadily across the rectangular black window - through all of the frequencies. Not a single word or a note of music was to be heard.

As Neville and Glynn tried to reassure Cynthia that she was not going to die, she lashed out and struck Clive in the face, and he started to cry. 'It's alright love, you're going to be okay! You're going to be fine!'

'I-can't – can't breathe! Help! Help me!' She gasped, her eyes bulging.

'Get her some water and sit her up!' Glynn suggested, and Hannah hurried into the kitchen. She couldn't get to the sink because Trevor was standing in it, and he was kicking the rest of the window in with his other foot, and this time parts of the frame splintered and came away.

'Trevor! Can you get out the way?' Hannah yelled,

and Trevor jumped down onto the kitchen floor as Harriet ran in.

'You can really see it now!' Trevor said with a look of horror, without even turning to acknowledge Harriet, who was shouting at him to stop destroying the window.

Hannah filled a glass with water from the tap and went into the living room, but now Cynthia was unconscious and Clive was hysterical. 'She's dead! She's dead!' he kept shouting.

'She's not, mate,' Glynn told him, all matter-of-fact, 'she's passed out, that's all!'

Trevor came into the living room and went to the telephone.

'It's dead,' Neville told him, with a look of resignation on his gaunt face.

Trevor picked up the handset anyway. There wasn't even a purring tone. He dialled 100 and begged God to put the operator in touch with him. Nothing.

There was a scream from the kitchen. It was Harriet's scream.

Neville bolted for the kitchen and saw Harriet with her hands on her face, and she was staring in horror at the smashed window.

'What?' Neville asked, and he could feel his heart palpitating now.

'The cat jumped out the window!' Harriet said, and when she got this upset she always made a retching sound. As long as Neville had known his partner, she had always exhibited this involuntary spasm of ineffectual vomiting when something shocked or sickened her. He ran to the window and put his head out. There was nothing to be seen below; just never-ending blackness.

'Are you *sure* he jumped out?' Neville asked, not wanting to believe Marmalade had gone into that awful sinister void.

Harriet was in tears as she nodded, and then she blamed Trevor for the loss of her cat, and she charged at him and began to pound his face and chest with her fists. Trevor pushed her away and Neville held her back.

'You can't blame me for that!' Trevor cried, stunned at the assault, 'You should have kept your eye on it!'

'My cat!' Harriet wandered into the living room, fell onto an armchair and bent into a foetal position, sobbing and shaking. 'I want my cat back...'

'Hail Mary, full of grace, the Lord is with thee, blessed...' Glynn was hugging Hannah tight, and he was praying as she nuzzled against his chest.

A strange silence then descended, and only Glynn's praying could be heard.

The television set exploded into a supernova of amplified sound and a picture appeared on the screen. Simultaneously the midi radio blasted out the inane voice of a Radio 1 DJ.

Glynn, who was kneeling besides the sofa, squeezing the hand of his unconscious wife, noticed the snowflakes falling past the window in the living room, and felt an enormous relief.

Trevor went to the front door and tried to open it. It was jammed. Glynn came over and realised that the catch was on, so he casually took it off, and opened the front door. Glynn immediately carried his wife outside and placed her on the thin dusting of snow on the garden lawn. And Marmalade came from the bush under the window and sniffed Cynthia's face as her eyelids flickered.

'Harriet?' Glynn rushed back into the living room and told Harriet the cat was alright.

Harriet gave a confused look, then wiped her streaming mascara with a paper hankie, shot up from the armchair and ran into the hallway. Marmalade passed her as he hurried to the warmth of the living room. She chased after him, and she hugged the cat and kissed him as only a female is allowed to by a feline.

All of the guests soon made excuses to leave, and all of them seemed afraid of even stepping back in the cottage in case that terrifying blackness enveloped the dwelling again. Trevor was the last to leave, and before he did he promised he'd pay for the damage to the kitchen window, and he apologised to Harriet and kissed and hugged her so tight she thought he'd cracked one of her ribs.

By one in the morning, Neville had tacked a board over the smashed window in the kitchen, and he was ready for bed. He made love to Harriet that night, and when he awoke around three in the morning he looked at the window, and for a moment he saw that it was very dark out there. A single whirling snowflake which drifted past the pane reassured him everything was okay. 'I love you,' he whispered to his sleeping partner.

'I know,' she said.

The voice didn't sound like her voice.

Neville reached out and clicked on the bedside light. He looked closely at her. She wasn't messing about; she seemed to be really sleeping. 'Harriet? You okay?'

'It isn't Harriet,' said the low voice. It sounded like a

foreign voice, but Neville could not place what country it belonged to.

'Stop messing about,' Neville said, and he got out the bed and walked around it then knelt at Harriet's side and took a good look at her face. Her eyes were swivelling from side to side under her lids – rapid-eye movement - which meant she was dreaming.

'This isn't Harriet,' she told him.

'Who are you then?' Neville asked, feeling very uneasy now, and a little sick because he hadn't had much sleep.

'That would only spoil the game,' said the voice.

'Harriet?' Neville shook his wife, and she awoke with a start.

'What? What! What is it?' she'd had a nightmare of Trevor killing Marmalade with the axe.

'You were talking in your sleep,' Trevor told her, and she could see how worried he was.

'Oh,' she said with a weak attempt at a smile, and closed her eyes. She dozed off again.

Neville got back into bed, switched off the night, and said, 'Night.'

'Night night,' said *that* voice again.

The bedside lamp went back on, and now Neville could feel his heart thrumming away. He shook his head, unable to believe what he was hearing. 'You okay, Harriet?' he asked, and expected the creepy voice to reply, but it never did.

Over a late breakfast on Boxing Day, Neville tried to tell Harriet he thought something strange was going on but his cousin, Arthur, who was a glazer, was hammering away, fitting a new window frame. By the late afternoon when the job was finally done, Neville suddenly remembered the two men who had called at the cottage yesterday – and how the one who had reminded him of Shoestring had claimed that something 'nasty' had sneaked into the cottage because he had left the door open. It all made some sense now. Neville told Harriet about the unearthly voice she had spoken in as he'd held a conversation with her while she was still asleep, but she said she'd been overtired and that the 'supernatural' blackness which had seemingly surrounded their home was probably caused by hysteria, stiff locks and an unusually thick fog.

'No,' Neville shook his head. 'And what about the telly and the radio and the phone all acting up?'

'I think you like trying to scare me, Neville,' Harriet said in a huff, and went upstairs to the toilet. From the landing up there she shouted down: 'I love you though. Let's put all last night behind us now.'

That night, the same thing happened. While Harriet was asleep, he held a full conversation with her – or *was* it her? Once again he asked the voice to identify itself, and this time it said, 'Wouldn't you like to know?'

'Yes, that's why I have just asked you,' Neville said with great impatience. 'Tell me who you are.'

'No,' said the voice, and Neville thought he heard a faint chuckle.

'Are you some sort of demon?' he asked, and it was a question he dreaded the answer to.

'Ask me anything, go on,' said the sinister voice, and Neville watched Harriet's little lips move as this thing spoke through her.

'What are you?'

'No, ask me anything but that,' the voice told him.

'Why are you speaking through Harriet?'

'Ask me anything but that, go on, and I'll tell you things you didn't know.'

'What are you?'

'Ask me anything but that, go on.'

'Did you have something to do with that blackness? The blackness that surrounded this cottage?'

'Ask me anything but that.'

'This is getting really annoying,' Neville rubbed his forehead. He was getting a headache over his left eye; it felt as if someone was inserting a knitting needle into his brain.

'Ask me anything, go on.'

'What's the square root of one hundred?' Neville asked, and he knew Harriet could not add up or do any form of arithmetic to save her life, but in a flash the voice said: 'Ten.'

'How many hairs have I got on my – '

'One hundred and sixty-five thousand, three hundred and twenty eight.'

' – head?'

The voice laughed.

'You could have just made that up,' Neville reasoned.

'I can tell you how many days you've lived and how many you have left if you want?'

'How many days have *you* got left to live?' Neville asked.

'Ask me anything but that, go on.'

'Why is God more powerful than evil?'

No reply came.

'Our father, who art in Heaven, hallow be thy name; thy kingdom…'

'Rubbish! Be quiet Neville!'

'I believe in God, and God will get rid of you!'

'"Oh, you can't help that," said the Cat: "we're all mad here. I'm mad. You're mad." '

Neville had heard those words a long time ago, but where? He suddenly realised where – his late grandmother had read *Alice's Adventures in Wonderland* to him as a little boy, so long ago. The thing was quoting Lewis Carroll.

'Lord, please remove this thing from Harriet – please Lord,' Neville pressed his palms together and looked up at the ceiling, earnestly meaning every word.

'Piss off, Neville!' said the voice and it sounded quite irritated.

'Lord, please send this thing back to where it came from!' Neville shouted, and he turned to look at his sleeping sweetheart, the girl who was literally his world, and he was almost in tears.

'Piss-baby tears!'

'Lord I love her, and I beg you to take this thing from out of her and destroy it!' Neville could hardly see Harriet now as a flood of stinging tears obscured his vision.

'Oh!' the voice sounded as if it was hurt. 'Oh!'

Neville wiped his eyes with the back of his hand and looked at Harriet. Her left eyelid opened, not with a swift curving motion, but as if something was pushing it open – from inside.

'Lord please get rid of this thing in Harriet,' Neville prayed, and felt a strange optimism welling up in his heart. He had never been near a church since the christening of his niece two years ago, and he was not a particularly religious man, but he felt as if God was there with him now, and he was sure He would rid Harriet's body of this weird entity.

Something which looked jet black and snakelike shot out of Harriet's left eye, and it landed silently on the bed, and then it fell onto the floor, and within a split second, Neville could see that dark long entity darting across the bedroom carpet – heading to the door. It went through the little gap under the door, and at that moment, Harriet awoke with a start and screamed. She sat upright in the bed and began to breathe heavily, and Neville tried to calm her down. 'It's alright love, it's alright!'

'I had a horrible nightmare,' Harriet said, and then she burst into tears in his arms. She couldn't even recall what the bad dream had been about but she knew it had been something absolutely horrific. Neville never mentioned what had happened that night for many years, for he thought the thing might return. He told Glynn what had happened and how it probably tied in with that frightening darkness which had surrounded the cottage and almost driven everyone insane. Glynn was a religious man, and he researched the history of the cottage Neville and Harriet lived in and unearthed a very unsavoury tale. In the 1870s, a reverend had lived in the cottage, and on Christmas Eve, several terrified villagers said a turkey which had been due to have its neck wrung had started spouting blasphemous words, and the family it belonged to were terrified of it. A farmer had tried to shoot it but his shotgun misfired and blasted off his toes. The turkey had gone on the run from its enclosure and a group of villagers with flaming torches had gone after it with pitchforks, rocks and clubs. The evil spirit possessing the bird had not only spouted scripture, but also lines from the fantasy book *Alice in Wonderland*. Neville went cold when Glynn told him this.

The possessed turkey had also accused a well-respected man of rape – and it transpired that this man had indeed committed a disgusting outrage on a young woman some years before – but he had evaded capture and had not been brought to justice. The accused man later committed suicide after the bird spouted its eerie claims about him. The turkey also seemed to know the secrets of every villager and was somehow aware of every family's skeleton in the cupboard. The reverend had therefore been sought out to exorcise the bird, and at first he refused, thinking it was all some seasonal hoax. A man named Williams, who was a local religious fanatic, urged the reverend to cast the evil demon out of the turkey, and in the end the reverend gave in and confronted the alleged possessed turkey in a barn. The bird never uttered a word or acted strange, and the reverend grabbed it – and he killed it by wringing its neck.

The family wanted to bury the bird rather than eat it for Christmas dinner, but the reverend, mindful of how hard the times were, and of the many poor people in the village who were going hungry, promised the family that there was nothing wrong with the turkey – and to prove it he promised to eat some of the bird himself. He subsequently took the cooked turkey from the hob in the kitchen of the local inn and after the meat had rested for twenty minutes he donned an apron before a crowd of bystanders and picked up a large carving knife and a steel sharpening rod. He theatrically stroked the blade of the knife up and down the sharpener, and then he cut off a piece of the turkey crown. Before the nervous and fascinated faces of the superstitious locals he threw back his head and dropped the slice of succulent white meat into his open mouth, and the holy man then closed his eyes, relishing it. He then offered other cuts of the bird to some of the hungriest-looking children present, but they all refused – and no one else would touch that cooked turkey. And on the next day in the midst of a sermon during the Christmas Mass, the reverend's face went pale, his eyes bulged, and his hair – which was always oiled and neatly parted – suddenly flew up as if he had seen a ghost. 'So, we *must believe* in Jesus! We must have faith!' the reverend intoned, and smoothing his hair back down as laughter rippled through the congregation, he continued his sermon. 'We must believe – why, sometimes I've believed as many as six impossible things before breakfast!'

This was recognised by the well-read members of the congregation as a quote from *Alice's Adventures in Wonderland*.

'Have I gone mad?' the reverend yelled, and he lifted his cassock up – and urinated on the congregation from the pulpit. An elderly lady asked if the roof was leaking at first, and then a young lady, realising what the yellow liquid splashing on her face and new Christmas clothes was, almost fainted. After the shock of this depraved act subsided somewhat, a group of men stormed the pulpit, and two of them suspected that the reverend had become possessed. Every form of exorcism was attempted to rid the evil and mischievous spirit from his body, but no one could cast it out, and when any priest came near to affecting the entity, it would reveal some scandalous piece of information about someone present, causing great distraction and confusion. In the end the poor reverend had his ears plugged with wax and cotton and he was bound in ropes and left in the belfry as the church bells were continually rung for almost an hour. During that time, the reverend's excrement rained down on the bell ringers but they continued under strict orders from a bishop. It is known that a bell can drive out an evil spirit, along with the reading of various psalms, and that's where the phrase, 'by bell, book and candle' comes from – it is referring to the three most effective means of exorcism. It took nine priests three months to fully exorcise the spirit, which some believed to have been a 'ten-fold' murderer of women and children, according to two priests who elicited some information from the presence. The killer had read chapters of *Alice in Wonderland* and other books to children before smothering them or cutting their throats. Other people had been hanged for these murders and the real killer eventually went insane and hanged himself on Christmas Day. The people of the village were so afraid of the evil spirit returning they rarely mentioned the Christmas exorcism, but someone in the Church recorded the terrifying events in a diary.

After hearing this, Neville put crucifixes in every part of the cottage and slept with a bible under his pillow – and he still sleeps with the Holy Book under his pillow today.

TINSEL AND TIMESLIPS

Before the arrival of the digital watch and clock, all of the timepieces in the world did not measure time – but *space* instead; the hour, minute and second hands of a watch swept through 360 degrees of space on the face of the watch, and we took that as a representation of time that had elapsed. It was the same with the shadow of a pointer moving across a sundial. Even today with digital readouts from watches and alarm clocks, we are only measuring an agreed local time; if you travel away from home and cross into another time zone, you have to adjust your watch by turning it backwards or forwards an hour, and of course, in the world today, we have 24 time zones that encircle the globe, although some countries have what are known as non-standard time zones, some with a 30 to 45-minute offset. India, for example has a time zone 5 and a half hours ahead of Coordinated Universal Time. We have time zones because clocks in villages and towns across the world were once set to dusk and dawn, and were gauged by the rising and setting of the sun at a particular location. A few centuries ago, before the dawn of regular long-distance travel by rail and road, most people didn't realise it was a different time in a different place, but today in the jet age, we are only too well aware of certain countries being hours ahead or behind the country we are flying from. Again, the time zones are just measurements of distance and space, because even today in this age of technological marvels, physicists do not know *what* time is. We are 'taught' to tell the time, and we are also taught to understand the calendar, but still we don't really know what time is, and in most people's minds time is a little-questioned concept. Physicists know that time slows down on clocks that move at very high velocities (and this is called time dilation) and they know that time can be almost halted at Absolute Zero or minus two-hundred and seventy-three point five degrees Celsius. But what *is it* which is being slowed down? What actually is time? You may be thinking to yourself: 'Well, I know what time is – it's *this* moment right now. But that moment soon passes and it becomes a *past* moment. Einstein stated that time – the idea we humans have of yesterday, today and tomorrow - is an illusion, and a very stubborn one at that. Modern physicists believe that all special moments – ones you had yesterday, ones you have now and ones you *will* have in the future, are all equally real, even though, to your present perception, yesterday seems to have *gone* and tomorrow has yet to *arrive* or *take place*, a scientist will not look at it that way – he or she will look at yesterday, today and tomorrow as mere points on a line, and they are all in existence. This goes against what we think of as Common Sense, but Common Sense isn't always correct. If you rap your knuckle on a table it seems solid enough to your sense of touch, even though that table is mostly made up of empty space and a host of vibrating subatomic particles. Some physicists think that time may not even exist outside of the human brain, that its just a mental process for making sense of events and bringing order to a chaotic universe. I personally think time *does* exist and that one day we will be able to manipulate it just as we leaned how to manipulate the wind to drive sailing ships across the world. There are so many questions about time that boggle the mind, but great discoveries often start with simple questions. The deceptively simple questions are: *what* actually keeps time moving forward? What propels the arrow of time from the past into the future? If I could reverse time so you rise from your grave and end up entering the womb of your mother feet first, your mind would accept this as normal, and you'd think nothing of regurgitating a cake from your mouth onto a plate, where it forms a perfect slice of gateau, and your coffee would get warmer and warmer (thus contravening the *forward* version of the Laws of Thermodynamics), but of course, time moves in the other direction – the direction we are accustomed to – from the past into the future - and no one knows why this is so. Nor do physicists know why time on a fast-moving clock slows down. In an experiment carried out by physicists Joseph C. Hafele and astronomer Richard E. Keating in 1971, it was discovered that an atomic clock flown around the world in a high-speed jet airliner lost 59 nanoseconds (compared to a stationary atomic clock on the ground at the United States Naval Observatory) when it travelled eastwards, but that same clock *gained* 273 nanoseconds when it was flown westwards in the same airliner travelling at a high speed. It was later worked out that the discrepancy was down to the rotation of the earth – that as the earth rotates towards the east, it added its rotational velocity to the velocity of the airliner. Furthermore, another major factor in the equation is gravitational potential - as altitude increases, the atomic clocks speed up as they get further from the pull of the earth, because gravity affects the flow of time; a clock ticking in one of the five basements of the One World Trade Center in New York will tick (fractionally) slower than a clock on the 104th floor. The most accurate atomic clocks have discovered that time slows down by 90 millionths of a second with every 12 inches you rise from the earth, and the One World Trade Center is 1,776 feet tall – so you do the math!

Einstein predicted this effect – that altitude affects the flow of time - back in 1905 in his original paper on Special Relativity, but not every scientist in those days could accept that this finding meant in effect that his head was ageing faster than his feet, according to this strange claim of Einstein, although the effect has been proved over and over again with atomic clocks since then. It now therefore seems likely that if gravity can be understood and controlled, it will not only provide us with a clean and novel propulsion system, it will undoubtedly provide us with the basis of a time machine. It would appear that, under certain circumstances we do not yet understand, time sometimes seems to *slip* so that 2015 becomes 1815 – and people have found themselves in the past or future. Science fiction films and novels have used the timeslip as a convenient dynamic trick to advance the storyline, and yet there have been quite a number of well-authenticated timeslips throughout history, and I have even experienced them myself. Some years ago I awoke in my bedroom and noticed that the curtains and décor were all wrong, and instead of double glazing on the window I had old fashioned window panes which were much broader and higher than the window I was accustomed to seeing there. The drapes were heavy and went to the floor, and my duvet now felt like linen blankets. The bed had changed too from a modern featureless one with a square white headboard to one with carved wooden bedposts and an intricate headboard. The light that normally shone into my room through the window had been a dreary sodium lamp, but now I could see the lantern of a gas lamp with a flickering flame. I closed my eyes – looked again – and the old-fashioned bed and backdated lamp post was still outside. I slowly realised I was experiencing a timeslip. I closed my eyes and waited for a while, perhaps about twenty seconds, then opened my eyes – and saw that the room had reverted back to normality. It's easy to explain the timeslip away as me being half asleep, but I was 100% sure that I had been awake at the time, but why my bedroom went back to what looked like the Victorian or Edwardian era is inexplicable to me. Other people – from all walks of life – have had much more dramatic experiences of a timeslip. What follows are just a couple of these timeslips, and in keeping with the theme of this book, the ones I have chosen all occurred around the Christmas period.

In December 1973, an elderly man named Mr Squirrel (not his real name), who lived on the coast of

Norfolk, decided to travel to Great Yarmouth to a corner shop – owned by a John Buckle (a well-known printer and bookbinder) - which sold general stationery items. Mr Squirrel was a coin-collector – or a numismatist to give him the official title – and he wished to obtain several coin envelopes of the plastic variety to store his coin collection in, and so, upon the recommendation of a friend he visited the corner shop, which he had seen in passing but had never visited before. When Mr Squirrel arrived at the shop he thought the cobbled space in front of the premises was dated but quaint, and the façade of the place also seemed to have been painted rather gaudily since he had last set eyes on it. He went inside and noted that the shop had photograph frames with floral features, a cylinder full of walking sticks and instead of a modern till, the shop had a rather old fashioned till-box. It was a case of 'anything goes' as regards to the fashion in 1973, and so, when the young assistant came through a doorway from the back of the shop wearing a long black skirt and a blouse with mutton-chop sleeves, Mr Squirrel merely thought the female assistant was following some latest fashion fad, as he certainly didn't keep up with the latest trends. The woman did have her hair done up in a bun though and this added to her 'vintage' look, but still the penny didn't drop. Mr Squirrel did notice one odd thing though; since he had entered the stationers a strange hard silence had descended on the place, and he could not hear the hubbub of the traffic outside.

'I'm looking for little envelopes to keep my coins in,' Mr Squirrel addressed the lady, who looked as if she was about twenty-one perhaps, and she reached for a small brown wooden box and opened it. From the box the shop assistant took some little envelopes out but they didn't look like they were the plastic ones Mr Squirrel had wanted. 'The men from the sailing ships use these to as receptacles for their fish hooks,' the assistant told Squirrel with a sombre-sounding voice.

'Ah,' was all the numismatist could say, a bit disappointed at the envelopes not being plastic.

'That will be one shilling, sir,' the assistant said.

Mr Squirrel still mentally calculated monetary value in the old pre-decimal money system, as a lot of people his age did in those days, and so he thought nothing strange of the mention of a shilling, but assumed she meant five pence – the shilling's modern equivalent, and he put the 5p in her soft white palm.

The lady behind the counter looked at the modern decimal coin with an expression of mild bafflement for a moment, and then Mr Squirrel said goodbye and walked out of the shop, and the sounds of the traffic assaulted his ears. Squirrel decided he liked the little quaint-looking coin envelopes after all, and so, days later, he returned to the shop – and he immediately notice that the cobbles in front of the premises that he had seen upon the last visit were now gone, and instead there was a stretch of pavement there. The garish façade he had seen last time had now gone, and instead the sign read: John Buckle Printers Ltd.

Mr Squirrel went into the shop and immediately noticed that the fixtures and layout of the shop were now different from the shop he had visited. Gone were the photograph frames with floral embellishments, the cylindrical holder of walking sticks and the quaint old till. A mature lady who bore no resemblance to the young woman who had served him last time stood behind the counter. 'Where's the young lady who served me last time?' he asked. 'Is it her day off?'

The shop assistant returned a black stare. 'Sorry?' she said.

Mr Squirrel told the woman about the girl who had served him last time and he produced a few of the little envelopes he had purchased from her.

The woman took a good look at the coin envelopes and then said that the shop had never stocked them, and, moreover, no young lady had ever worked at John Buckle Ltd.

'Are you sure?' Mr Squirrel asked, rather confused by this unsettling information.

The manager was brought out to see Mr Squirrel and he assured him that the shop assistant was being truthful. Mr Squirrel made enquiries and showed the coin envelopes to experts, and they confidently told him that the type of envelopes he had purchased dated back to the 1920s but the method of manufacturing them was known in a few places before the First World War. Only then did Mr Squirrel realise that through some inexplicable slip in time he had visited a shop in the past – possibly the Edwardian era – to buy those coin envelopes and he had not even been aware of this strange fact at the time.

In the world of the occult, it is said that sometimes an event happens which is so tragic or horrific, it casts a shadow ahead of itself in time which is perceived by some sensitives as a kind of premonition. The following story features such a horrific incident which was foreseen by two people back in 1957.

Experimental TV transmissions started as early as 1934 in Brisbane, Australia, but officially, commercial television began in earnest in Australia in 1956, when Melbourne and Sydney became the first cities in the country to enjoy widespread ownership of TV sets and one Melburnian, a 35-year-old electronics hobbyist and amateur short-wave radio enthusiasts named Rod Jones, not only owned one of the first monochrome sets, he also tinkered with it, adding his own home-made aerial booster to drag in broadcasts from around the world. Rod erected a sixty foot TV aerial in the backyard of his home in Carlton, a suburb of Melbourne, and at first all he received were pictures from HSV-7, Melbourne's first TV station, but after adding more sensitive circuits to his aerial amplifier, he began to pick up clear television transmissions from Britain – twelve thousand miles away - which astounded him and a few of his friends who were into long-distance radio. Rod picked up *Hancock's Half Hour*, a dramatisation of Guy de Maupassant's *The Diamond Necklace*, *Panorama* a current affairs documentary programme, and *Gun Law* a Western drama series (later renamed *Gunsmoke*).

Rod and his friends also saw what appeared to be a horrifying film about a train crash which actually showed crushed, maimed and dismembered bodies and featured blood-curdling screams. Rod's wife, who had been up a step ladder putting up the Christmas decorations, was badly affected by the pictures of the crash and almost fainted at the sight of so much gore on the TV screen. She said she believed it was not a show at all but actual footage of a real-life train smash that some irresponsible idiot had broadcast. That transmission was picked up on Monday, 2 December 1957, and Rod wrote it down in his log book. He then set about trying to increase the sensitivity of the amplifier signal booster circuit, and a few days later, he got the shock of his life, because the news reached Australia of a horrific train crash at Lewisham in South East London. While it was sweltering in Melbourne, London had been experiencing a freezing fog on the evening of Wednesday 4 December that year, and by 5pm it had thickened and settled in the Thames Basin, reducing visibility to about ten yards. The thick 'pea souper' fog not only brought traffic in the capital to a virtual standstill, it also affected the running of the rail network because the train drivers could not see the signals clearly. As a consequence of the fog then, many of the trains were running out of order and up to forty minutes late, like the one due at Charing Cross station. Among the dozens of complaining passengers waiting at that station that Wednesday evening, there were a young engaged couple named Ronald and Betty. They had spent the day doing a bit of early Christmas shopping for their families, but Betty was a bit upset as she stood on the platform stamping her feet in the cold. Earlier in the day she and her fiancé had been accosted at a café by a woman who professed to be a gypsy, and she had read the palms of the couple. The woman had said Betty would have many children but refused to say whether those children would be Ronald's. To make matters worse, the palm reader had told Ronald that there was a dark-haired lady who had been around him an awful lot of late and this woman would meet Ronald very soon. Ronald had a peculiar look in his eye as the gypsy told him this, and after courting Ronald for three years, Betty knew that look so well; it meant that he was hiding something. 'You will catch her eyes,' the gypsy told him, and then she left the café after taking a ten bob note from Ronald.

'You know who this woman is, don't you?' Betty had asked him, and Ronald had tried to make light of the gypsy's forecast, but then he had admitted that for the last fortnight he had been continually noticing a particular dark-haired woman of about thirty on almost a daily basis. He had seen her on buses, on trains, in the library, in several shops, 'And the weird thing is that I sort of get this hunch which tells me I'm going to bump into her,' Ronald had told Betty.

Betty really loved Ronald. She'd been engaged before in her teens and nothing became of it, but this time she really hoped she'd make it to the altar. 'Is she better looking than me?' Betty had asked, and Ronald had laughed and told her she was obviously jealous about a woman he did not even care for.

'But the gypsy said you'll catch her eyes, and that doesn't sound good to me,' Betty told him, and seemed very tearful.

Ronald had tried to reassure her. 'Betty, I only love you, and I only want you, and when we save a little bit we can get married, hopefully next year. Stop worrying, dear.'

And now here they were at what should have been the end of a lovely day out, despite the icy fog, but Betty was still sulking as she stood on the platform with Ronald, who would soon have to leave his sweetheart to go home. The train eventually came to take him home to Hayes, and he kissed Betty and told her he'd see her tomorrow evening.

'Don't you run off with that dark-haired woman,' Betty told him as he boarded the packed train.

Ronald laughed and waved to his fiancée – but all of a sudden he had that feeling – the feeling he always got when that dark-haired lady was about – and he looked around the crowded carriage – and there she was. She was standing in the middle of the carriage which was jam-packed with commuters and early Christmas shoppers. As the train moved off, Ronald wondered where the lady would get off. The train progressed through all of the familiar stations: Waterloo, London Bridge, New Cross…

It was 6.20pm, when the train suddenly stopped because of a warning light barely visible up ahead in the fog. The train waited there in an eerie silence beneath the Nunhead flyover, a bridge of 350 tons of steel. The train Ronald was on was electric and made up of 10 coaches crowded with rush-hour travellers and Christmas shoppers such as himself, and they all wondered why their train had stopped. Someone thought they heard something; it sounded like another train approaching – from behind. It sounded like a steam train.

The driver of this steam train, which had come from Canon Street station, bound for Ramsgate, suddenly saw to his horror, that there was a stationary train in his path. He slammed on the brakes, and sparks flew from the moist, icy rails as the metal wheels tried to get a grip, but it was too late. The steam train ploughed into the back of the stationary train and also swung sideways. It struck one of the steel columns supporting the flyover, and what followed was the stuff of nightmares. The 350 ton steel bridge fell onto Ronald's train, almost pulping the bodies of 90 passengers in two carriages and injuring over a hundred. A train had been about to cross the fallen bridge but had just managed to stop in time. All the same, the scene below was one of absolute carnage. Screams that were heard for miles had an eerie echo to them below that crumpled bridge, and what seemed like gallons of blood had sprayed out of the crushed carriages that had been packed with people just wanting to get home out of this terrible fog. Just before the lights went out in his carriage, Ronald saw the woman with the dark hair being horrifically crushed by a massive steel girder which smashed open her skull, throwing her brain out of her head in the process into the face a terrified old lady, and the young woman's yes also flew out in the sickening impact, and Ronald, lifting his hands reflexively to shield himself from the collapsing roof and the crushed bodies, somehow caught her ejected eyeballs in each hand, and then he collapsed, more from shock than a physical injury. When he came to he found himself caked in the blood and body fluids of people – and some of them had literally been pressed flat. When the torch-beams of rescuers came raking through the fog which had even infiltrated the wreckage, Ronald discovered he could not feel his right leg. It was broken, but he was thankful he was still alive. A man in a trilby could be seen in silhouette, near to a gaping hold in the wall of the carriage, and he appeared to be standing up, but when the torchlight fell momentarily upon him, Ronald could see the man was standing there with his hands clasped in prayer – with a six-foot length of metal protruding a few feet out the centre of his chest. The other bodies were grotesquely mixed up with the debris and the floor of the carriage was ankle-deep in the blood of the crash victims. The poor old lady who'd had her face splattered with that woman's brains lay there with her face contorted in agony, and her little body was bisected just below the chest where her mackintosh had been torn to shreds by sheets of metal rammed into her in the deadly impact. She was just one of ninety who perished that night in December 1957. Strangely enough, there had been another Lewisham train crash one hundred years before in 1857. As Ronald recovered from his broken leg at home days later, he told Betty the way he had caught that unknown woman's eyes during the grotesque accident, and realised what the gypsy had meant when she had told him: 'You'll catch her eyes.'

The brush with death made Ronald realise how precious life was, especially with Betty, and that Christmas he bought her all sorts of gifts and they stayed together at a hotel. The couple married two years later and the couple produced nine children – so it looks as if that gypsy woman's other prediction – about Ronald having lots of children – had also been accurate.

It is said that on certain foggy nights, always in December, the terrible screams of the victims of the Lewisham train disaster are heard near to the place where they lost their lives; it's as if time is replaying the tragedy for some warped reason, or perhaps the ghosts of the dead are still not at rest and they are just yearning to go home.

And now we move forward a few years to the Christmas of 1961, and we venture north across the land till we come to the grim majesty of Glencoe, one of Scotland's most wild but celebrated glens, the scene of the notorious massacre of the MacDonald clan in February 1692. Well, the history books say it was a massacre, but it could be called a wholesale 'murder under trust'. A company of 135 soldiers under the command of 60-year-old Captain Robert Campbell of Glenlyon had been billeted with the MacDonalds for a fortnight at Glencoe. The soldiers treated the MacDonalds like family; they played games with the little children, respected the old folk, and many a soldier cast a lustful eye upon the young MacDonald women, and they all ate and slept together, civilian and soldier. And then the militia turned into cold-blooded murderers overnight after a chilling message was received by Captain Campbell from a captain Drummond. The shocking instructions were from Major Duncanson, Campbell's superior officer. Campbell was to kill the MacDonalds; he was to 'cut off these miscreants root and branch,' and Campbell read the rest of the disturbing missive. It instructed him to 'put all to the sword [who are under the age of] seventy', and he was to do it in a surprise attack at 5am while his kind hosts would all be sleeping in their beds. Captain Campbell, a drunken shambles of a man who had only accepted his commission to pay off his gambling debts, went ahead with the massacre, but some of his officers broke the blades of their swords rather than kill the very people they had lived with in such a cowardly way. One soldier was so sickened by the order to kill a woman and her crying baby, he let them go and ran his sword through a wolf so he could show the bloodstained blade to his officer as proof of his unquestioning obedience. Some of the MacDonalds were allowed to escape as the sympathetic soldiers turned a blind eye, but Captain Campbell made sure the homes of the MacDonalds were burned down, and so forty women and children died of exposure as they wandered in shock in the snowy wastes. Now, under Scottish Law, there is a special category for this type of murder, and that is "Murder Under Trust" – and despite the military excuse for the massacre – that the King – William III – had signed the massacre order – the legal stance in Scotland was that this was no excuse for murder, and a type of murder which almost bordered on what we would today call ethnic cleansing. The Clan Campbell were stained for evermore with the mark of Cain upon their lineage – and even today the memory of the despicable massacre of men women and children at Glencoe is still raw in some people's minds, and you will often see signs in Scottish inns that read: No Hawkers or Campbells. The massacre has also left an indelible stain upon the beautiful landscape of Glencoe which many psychics have picked up on over the centuries, and there have been reports of Campbells who have wandered through Glencoe – even in recent times – being found dead in some strange circumstances. Some people have claimed that weird "fairy pipers" have led tourists surnamed Campbell into the mountains where they have become hopelessly lost and disoriented, only to die from exposure or from terrible falls from ridges and into deep gullies. There is also an even more ancient supernatural menace which sometimes haunts the mountainous grandeur of Glencoe, and it stretches back into the mists of prehistory, long before the coming of the clans, to a forgotten epoch when Scotland was unnamed by the human tongue. Most people are not aware that Scotland is geologically alien to Europe because it is actually a lost part of a prehistoric continent named 'Laurentia' by modern geologists. Laurentia not only formed Scotland, but also North America, Canada and Greenland about 2 billion years ago. This was an aeon when the young continents of Earth moved about, smashing into one another in a speeded-up form of Continental Drift. Under certain conditions, a portal to those bygone geologically-violent aeons of unimaginable time seems to open up at Glencoe.

In September 1961 two men from Lancashire named Gareth and John – both aged twenty – decided to go camping at Glencoe, but their stay at the glen didn't last long, because hours after they pitched their tent, one of the worst thunderstorms in living memory broke out and two young campers just a mile away were struck dead as they slept when lightning hit the steel pole which supported their tent. The bodies of the young men, aged 22 and 25, were later found still in their sleeping bags. They'd died instantly in their sleep from electrocution. Gareth and John had to return home after the storm blew away their tent and left them to the mercy of strange oversized hailstones that pelted them and left them with bruised faces. The lads returned to Glencoe in December (just a few days before Christmas) and thought they might even try a bit of skiing, as snow is common from mid-December to as late as April at Glencoe, where the highest point is 3,766 feet. Gareth and John pitched their tent on the floor of the valley at Glencoe on the first night after shovelling away a thick crust of frozen snow. Despite the glacial cold, the young men managed a good night's sleep in their sleeping bags, aided with a few drams of whiskey, and upon the next morning, they got out the camping stove and had a breakfast of eggs, bacon, black pudding and sausages, as well as a flask of hot coffee. They then set out to climb Buachaille Etive Mòr – a mountain which rises to a height of 1,749 feet, but once again the unpredictable Caledonian weather thwarted the aims of the two men, and a thick fog of a strange bluish hue choked the glen, and Gareth and John became hopelessly lost. Then came the sounds of thunder, and this thunder rolled much longer than normal thunder and shook the ground violently. It went on for so long in fact, the lads were driven to distraction by it. Then they saw a faint glow in the distance, and when the fog thinned, they got the shock of their lives. A gigantic volcano lay misted in the distance, and seemed even higher than any mountain in Glencoe. It looked positively terrifying as it spewed out bright orange lava from its rim. Black billowing clouds of smoke were also pouring out of the volcano, and the tourists suddenly realised that this active volcano had been the source of the 'thunder', and the lads decided it was time to leave the area. They really believed that the volcano had just erupted in modern-day Scotland, and fled into the fog, but they could not find their way back to the tent and did not recognise any features of the strange terrain. They noticed the silhouette of a man at one point and headed towards him, and it turned out that this person was also lost like them. He looked about 21 or 22 years of age and said his name was David, and he spoke with a Scottish accent. David had also been camping on Glencoe, and had often come up here alone to 'get away from the rat race' he told Gareth and John. The three of them ended up walking in circles, and once again they could see the terrifying super-volcano in the distance, and it was now throwing out bright blobs of lava which resembled distress flares. David said that Glencoe had been a powerful volcano about 400-odd million years ago (and this is correct) and that it had last erupted in the Silurian period, when plants moved out of the sea onto land. Perhaps it had become active again, but if that was so, why had the surrounding area of Glencoe changed – apparently beyond recognition – and where had all the snow gone? The air seemed to be full of choking acidic fumes and the eyes of Gareth in particular, were badly affected. He could hardly see because of the tears welling in his eyes, and his nose also ran. David began to cough, and suggested that they should turn around and try to find another way to escape from the toxic emissions of the volcano. The three disoriented young men walked as far away from the ominous volcano as they could, although the noise from it was still ear-splitting. The blue fog Gareth and John had encountered earlier in the morning returned, and the three men almost lost sight of each other when the visibility dropped to within a few feet. Gareth and John somehow remained together, but when they looked about they could not see David.

And then they heard terrible screams, coming from their left. They ventured gingerly in the direction of the screams and saw what they first took to be a group of about twelve children, silhouetted against the fog. A pale light was now breaking through the mists, and when John looked up, he saw it was the moon breaking through. Two things did not make sense. What would a full moon be doing out in the morning at what would have been about eleven o'clock, and secondly, why did the moon look twice as near as it normally did? John noted that the lunar features looked odd too. He was an amateur astronomer and he could see that Mare Crisium was in the wrong place, as if the Moon had tilted off its usual axis.

Gareth dabbed his watering eyes with a handkerchief and looked at the children about a hundred and fifty yards away. As the fog began to thin, Gareth got the shock of his life, because he could now see that they weren't children at all, but small muscular hairy men, all about three to four feet in height, and they were wielding what looked like spears and clubs – and they were battering David, who had fallen to his knees, and some of the pygmy-like beings were stabbing him with the pointed poles they carried. John could clearly see the blood issuing out the ghastly wounds in David's chest and neck, and when the Scotsman held his hands out in a defensive manner, the hairy midgets cruelly pierced the palms with quick stabs from their spears.

To their everlasting shame, Gareth and John turned and ran, and were glad to see the rolling fog ahead, for they would use it as a cover. As they ran to heaven knows where they heard the agonised shrieks and screams suddenly come to an abrupt halt far behind them, as if David had just been killed.

All of a sudden, Gareth and John, in their blind panic, ran straight over a ridge and fell for about thirty feet, and when they landed, they found themselves on a snowy slope. The fog had completely lifted but the skies were grey and darkening. There was a fierce hail shower and the men eventually found their tent. When they checked their watches, they discovered that the time was almost four in the afternoon. They had both lost about five hours. They packed up then and there, and eventually found a tiny hotel where they lodged for the remainder of that day before getting the train back to Lancashire. They told no one about their strange experiences for years, but were intrigued when they later learned that there had been many timeslips at Glencoe. People have seen the ghosts of the Glencoe Massacre of 1692 there, and there have also been sightings of the unidentified volcano. If this phantom volcano is not some mirage, but a genuine apparition, it must be one of the oldest 'ghosts' in history dating back 420 million years - for that is when a volcano of that size existed at Glencoe. Strange thunder is still occasionally heard at Glencoe, even when the weather is fine, and on one occasion in February 1970, a deafening roll of 'thunder' caused an avalanche. On that occasion a supersonic boom from Concorde was blamed - even though Concorde was not in the air at that time. Was the explosive sound caused by that ancient supervolcano erupting aeons ago, and sending its thunder through the time-barrier to the present?

And what of the strange tribe of little hairy men Gareth and John saw that December day? No one knows who or what they are – or *were* – but there have been many reported encounters of such hairy midgets over the years at Glencoe (and they have often been classed by the superstitious as Brownies, elves or Kobolds). Gareth and John still have nightmares about that apparent timeslip in Scotland, and they wonder if David somehow found his way back to 1961, or was he murdered – and possibly even eaten by some prehistoric tribe of diminutive cannibals in the remote past?

BOBBY

In 2012 I received an interesting letter from Frank Whittaker, a reader of my column about the supernatural in the *Liverpool Echo*. Frank asked me if I had ever heard about a weird 'boy' named Bobby in the late 1960s who was feared as a type of bogeyman character. The mere mention of this boy's name was enough to send a shudder down your spine, according to Frank. I was then on a local radio programme talking about paranormal incidents which had happened locally, and I asked anyone listening to phone me at the station or to email me if they knew anything about a strange boy named Bobby who, despite being about five feet tall, was pushed about in a pram by his eccentric mother. The radio station was deluged with calls as a result and I received dozens of emails and letters, and all of them confirmed Frank's letter and expanded on his account. Here's what I gleaned from the communications.

In 1968 there was a strange woman who used to go round Liverpool City Centre, often pushing a boy of about 10 about in a large black pram. Bemused passers-by would peep into the hood of the pram when the woman would always ask them to have a look at her 'lovely son Bobby fast asleep'. The boy in the pram looked eerily unreal, as if he was a shop-window dummy or some oversized doll, and his eyes in particular looked lifeless. The uncanny-looking boy always wore a red woollen hat with a bobble on it, a dark blue coat to his knees, unmatched woollen gloves, yellowish trousers and dark red shoes that looked more suited to girls. Frank Whittaker was only 12 when he first encountered Bobby one snowy day, walking along Cropper Street (behind the city's world-famous Lewis's store). Frank, a lad from the Paddington area of the city, was with a gang of mates, and they all started to snowball Bobby, and he began to hurl snowballs back at them. One of the gang silently crouched behind Bobby and another one hit him squarely in the face with a snowball with a stone concealed within its nucleus. The boy toppled backwards, fell flat in the snow and lay there, motionless. When the gang looked at the boy close up, he had his eyes wide open and his face looked plastic. The boy's mother came on the scene screeching at the boys, and then she picked up Bobby and stuffed him into the pram. 'My son will be the first man on the moon one day,' she said, and all of the gang laughed and ran off.

A local newsagent named Jack was creeped out by the artificial-looking boy. Bobby would come into his shop with a list in one gloved hand and coins wrapped in paper in the other. He would give Jack the list of items his mother wanted, usually pipe tobacco, a newspaper and a bag of sweets. Jack would then hand the change and the items down to Bobby – who would never utter a word before leaving the shop. Jack's wife, Muriel, was convinced that Bobby was a midget wearing a mask, but her husband thought there was something positively sinister about the boy. He felt that if that plastic mask was ripped off Bobby's face, something demonic would be exposed. Muriel laughed when he told her this, and she said, 'Oh don't be silly; it's just some dwarf messing about; I'll get to the bottom of this, you'll see.' And about a week after Muriel said Bobby came into the shop and once again he handed a little piece of paper upon which his 'mother' had written a list of items, including a newspaper, and on this occasion, a can of cat meat.

Out of burning curiosity, Muriel grabbed her coat and headscarf and she followed Bobby out of the shop to his home, which was not far from a huge tenement building known as the Bullring (or the "Bully"). Muriel noticed how Bobby was almost knocked down as he crossed roads in a mechanical fashion and never looked right or left. Dogs would either whine or run when they saw the boy coming or sometimes they would bark furiously at him – as if they knew he was not a real boy. And then one wintry afternoon in January 1969, Bobby was crossing London Road near Jerome the Photographer's shop, presumably on an errand again, when a petrol tanker ran him over. In the snow they found nothing but plastic jointed limbs and what looked like the head of a little shop-window manikin. Some disconcerting reports state that old human bones and scrolls with strange writing on were found in the crushed plastic and plaster shell of Bobby's body. The tanker driver swore he had seen a 'real living boy step out in front of him' – and a woman who had witnessed what she perceived as a real boy being knocked down was treated for shock. After the road accident, Bobby's "mum" took to wearing black funereal clothes and a black mantilla lace veil over her face for a period of mourning which lasted about three months. She continued to walk the streets of Liverpool – with the bits and pieces of Bobby in her pram, and still she would ask passers-by to look at her 'lovely son' fast asleep in the pram. Then, around Halloween, Frank Whittaker was challenged by one of his own gang members to do something which would prove he was the cock of the gang. Frank found a tin of whitewash in his backyard, and so he sneaked it out the yard, and he called on the gang, and he showed them the tin of cheap white paint and hid it in their den. He promised he would throw that tin of whitewash all over the barmy mother of Bobby – and he did. The poor unbalanced woman was walking down a street near to Bobby's house one evening, pushing the pram full of Bobby's remains, when Frank stepped out of an entry with a Lone Ranger mask on – and in his hand he held the tin of whitewash – minus its lid. 'Good evening love!' he shouted, and he threw the entire contents of that tin all over the woman, and it not only coated her head, face and coat with whitewash, it also went all over the black pram. The six members of the gang shrieked like chimps as they watched from the window of a nearby derelict house. As they all laughed, Frank hurled the emptied tin into the pram and ran for his life down the entry.

Bobby's make-believe mother screamed and she shouted at the top of her voice: 'I know who did that! I know who that bastard was! He'll wish he'd never been born!' And then she began to cry as she took the discarded tin of whitewash out of the pram. 'Oh! My Bobby! Bobby, are you alright love?' she groaned, and the gang in the condemned and empty house were rolling on the floor, laughing at the woman's concern for the remains of Bobby.

In December, "Bobby" appeared on the snowy streets of Liverpool one twilit afternoon on Shaw Street, and he looked ghastly. He had been glued and taped back together, and his face was disjointed, with one eye lower than the other and a long jagged fracture line running the length of his face. When Frank Whittaker's gang heard that the weird doll-like Bobby was roaming the streets again, they acted all tough and said they'd seek him out, but instead, Bobby found *them* – on Christmas Eve near London Road, the scene of his 'fatal' road accident the year before. The gang were having a snowball fight that day, and Frank Whittaker was being pulled along in the snow on his home-made sledge by his younger brother Tony – when he spotted Bobby. At first he thought someone had dressed up in clothes similar to Bobby just to scare him, for the figure was still about a hundred yards off, but Frank could still make out the red woollen hat and the blue coat.

Then as the figure drew nearer, and Frank could see that it *was* the terrifying ersatz boy, he got off his sledge and shouted to the members of his gang, and they were so afraid they all ran off home. Frank was so scared he left his beloved sledge behind and headed for the sanctuary of his grandma's house in Everton. He told his Gran what he had seen and she told him it was probably just some mischievous lad pretending to be that Bobby character. But then there was a heavy ran-tan on the door, and Bobby went to the window and looked out. It was Bobby, and although it was dark by now, he could see he was holding what looked like a huge carving knife. Bobby continued knocking heavily on the door - *ran-tan-tan-tan-tan...*

Frank Whittaker begged his grandmother not to let Bobby into the house but the old woman laughed and went into the hallway, then headed for the vestibule door, and as she did, Frank ran into the kitchen, and because he couldn't find the key to the door which led from the kitchen to the yard, he climbed onto the window ledge and climbed out the kitchen window, falling into the back yard where he almost broke his ankle as he landed hard in the snow. Whimpering, on the brink of bursting into tears, Frank slid back the bolt on the backyard door and he ran down the alleyway, slipping and falling in the snow several times. When he reached home, he had a stitch in his side, and he told his mother about Bobby visiting him at his grandmother's house – with the big knife. 'I'm warning you Frank,' his mother said with a suspicious look, 'If you're telling fibs – '

'Mam I'm not! He's back, and he had a big knife!' Frank told his mother, and he spat on the floor and said, 'I spit on our Tony's life! That Bobby thing's after me, Mam!'

'What would he want with *you* anyway?' Mrs Whittaker asked, and Frank wanted to confess to throwing that tin of whitewash over Bobby's 'owner' but he couldn't admit to it, as he knew his father would give him a hiding.

Mrs Whittaker told her husband the bizarre story, and he was a bit tipsy because he'd just been to the neighbours' house next door for a few Christmas Eve drinks. Mr Whittaker said he didn't believe his son but said he'd check on his mother-in-law anyway, just in case someone *had* called at her home with a knife. When Mr Whittaker got there he found the front door open and his mother-in-law was in tears, slumped in her armchair by the fire, surrounded by her neighbours. Mr Whittaker asked his mother-in-law what had happened and she said a boy in a mask with a knife had called at the house, and he had barged past her and began slashing the furniture with the knife as he looked about. 'He went upstairs and ripped the mattress on my bed and he seemed to be looking for something or someone,' Frank's Gran said, and sobbed. Then she told Mr Whittaker how the boy's face looked all disfigured and 'stuck together with plasters'. Mr Whittaker looked about and saw the frenzied slash-marks to the other armchair and even to the curtains. He suddenly sobered up when he saw this.

Fearing for his wife and son's safety, Mr Whittaker left the house immediately and went straight home. The shock had suddenly alerted his mind to the possibility that his son *had* been telling the truth, but who was this thug named Bobby? His wife asked him if her Mum was alright and when he told her about a boy slashing her furniture and bed, Mrs Whittaker became hysterical and wanted to go to the aid of her mother immediately. Frank Whittaker began to cry, and his father told him to shut up and went to put the bolt on the door.

'I want to go and see my mam,' Mrs Whittaker bawled and her husband told her that she was safe as houses with all her neighbours around her.

Frank then let out a ghastly scream and he had his

terrified eyes on the kitchen window. Through that window, Mr Whittaker could see a boy in a red woollen hat with a grotesque patchwork face, climbing over the backyard wall.

Frank's dad rushed to the kitchen door which led to the backyard and he put the bolts on. Frank and his parents stood in the kitchen and heard something rapping on the window. Through the frosted glass, they could all see a distorted image of that weird taped-up jigsaw of a face, and the knife tip was scraping the putty out of the glass now!

'Get in the parlour, come on!' Mr Whittaker shouted, and he opened the kitchen door and shoved his wife and son into the hallway. He opened the parlour door and told them to go in there and stay there. He then went back into the kitchen, and Frank and his mother could hear him getting something from the coal cellar before going up the stairs. Mrs Whittaker screamed when she heard the sound of breaking glass coming from next door in the kitchen.

Mr Whittaker went into the spare room, lifted the window open with great difficulty, then popped his head out and looked down into the yard. There was the accursed animated effigy, and there was a pane of broken glass on the window ledge. He would be able to climb into the kitchen now. Mr Whittaker unscrewed the top off the can of paraffin he'd fetched from the cellar and he quickly tilted the can so the spout of pink liquid arced out in a trajectory which splashed it all over that monstrosity. The red woollen hat was soaked, and then the paraffin splashed all over the thing's blue coat. The entire contents – half a can – were now ready to be ignited. Mr Whittaker lit a Swan

Vesta match and threw it down at the creepy effigy, but the match went out before it got anywhere near Bobby. Frank's father swore under his breath and took the handkerchief out of his top pocket and he picked up the can of pink paraffin and emptied what little was left of it into that cotton hankie, and then he lit it and it burst into a small blue fireball which singed an eyebrow. The handkerchief was dropped – and unlike the match it remained alight – and it hit the back of Bobby as he crawled into the kitchen. The doll, or effigy, or Golem, or whatever that thing was – burst into flames.

But still it crawled through the window and it began to search for Frank Whittaker, and clouds of black smoke filled the kitchen. Its burning gloved hand opened the door and it went into the hallway. By then, Mr Whittaker was halfway down the stairs, and he saw the burning boy walking along the hallway with his ignited woollen red hat dripping down his face as it melted. Choking black smoke blossomed upwards and Mr Whittaker had to leap down the stairs to get out of the way of the toxic fumes. He went into the coal cellar and came back out with the coal hatchet. As Bobby opened the parlour door, Mr Whittaker came behind it, and he could see his wife and son hiding under the table, looking at the flaming figure lunging forward with the huge knife. Mr Whittaker hacked the head of the simulacrum to bits with the hatchet, and with each strike, smoke and incandescent particles and bits of plaster flew in all directions. The screams under the table filled the ventricles of Mr Whittaker's heart with absolute terror of the kind he had never felt before, and he hit Bobby repeatedly until the thing had no head, and he pushed it sideways, and it fell over. Its legs kept moving backwards and forward robotically. Frank and his mother saw their chance and they ran out of the parlour and down the hallway to the front door. Frank heard his father shouting words and profanities he did not understand. Mr Whittaker whacked the imitation schoolboy until its right hand – the knife-wielding hand – came clean off. He then experienced what some soldiers in action have called the "red mist" – a strange state of consciousness where the combatant is acting on a type of autopilot. Mr Whittaker eventually realised he had turned the 'dummy' into dismembered parts and he had even destroyed the armchair next to the unearthly entity. Frank and his parents then went outside and they coughed and wheezed because of the smoke, and when Mr Whittaker realised what he had done, he felt his heart rise into his mouth, for he wondered if he had killed a real child in the frenzied attack on Bobby, so he went into the parlour, and he saw, without a doubt, that this thing had not been made of flesh and blood, but of plaster and plastic and god knows what.

The remains of Bobby were burnt in a pile in the backyard on Boxing Day, just in case his mother tried to resurrect him. The years went by and Frank Whittaker had recurrent nightmares about the little homunculus for years. When he was 19, Frank began to date a beautiful girl from Kensington, and one day he bought an engagement ring and went to her house to propose, and as he waited on the doorstep for his girlfriend to open the door, he saw a familiar woman passing by on the other side of the street. It was Bobby's mother, and she looked no different. She was pushing a pram. She didn't see Frank, and he averted his gaze and when his girlfriend opened the door he startled her by inviting himself in. Frank made out that he was just eager to ask her a question, and he proposed to her – and she accepted. The couple later married and Frank bought a little terraced house across the Mersey in Birkenhead, as far away from that weird woman and her 'son' as he could get!

THE CHRISTMAS BALL

The following story was related to me many years ago. It took place just before Christmas 1967. I have had to change a few of the names in this disturbing tale for legal reasons, but otherwise the events depicted in it are exactly as I describe.

Hadley Hampton-Pole - a 27-year-old layabout and drug-addict, and the black sheep of a well-off family who no longer had anything to do with him - was squatting at a 2-bedroom flat within a stone's throw of the affluent Holland Park area of London. He sat naked, cross-legged on a beanbag under a dreary bare fifty-watt light bulb, basking in the chilblained warmth of a two-bar electric fire with *Sergeant Pepper's Lonely Hearts Club Band* crackling along on his old 1950s record player. He had a joint in his mouth and despite his elongated consciousness he was trying to digest the five-shilling autumn edition of *Pentagram* magazine, which had a controversial feature in it by Alastair Crowley on 'the Psychology of Hashish'. It was 7pm and beyond the curtainless windows ghostly sleet was falling straight in the absence of any breezes on this chilly December night.

The door opened and in with a gelid draught came a willowy blonde in her early twenties carrying a bag made of large coloured beads the size of chestnuts and two bulging and garishly coloured plastic carrier bags. She smiled and shook her head gently in a dismissive manner when she saw her boyfriend sitting there in his birthday suit, and he looked up at her, red-eyed, and returned a weak smile. Astrid looked up at the tungsten filament bulb hanging from the ceiling, then turned her eyes to the electric fire and asked: 'Did your anarchist friend switch the electricity on then?'

'Yeah,' was all Hadley could manage, and he held his hand in the air and moved his fingers around with typical vagueness, saying: 'He did something with wires and that, and um, bypassed the meter and stuff.'

'Groovy,' said Astrid, and she put the big bead bag on the floorboards, coughed and waved her hands through the joint vapours before taking his costume out the first carrier bag. 'Didn't I tell you the best store for fancy dress is Nathan's of Drury Lane? I got you this,' she said and beamed a big attractive smile at him.

'Oh man! Wow!' Hadley loved the monk's outfit, a realistic hooded dark-brown cowl, and Astrid had even got hold of a pair of monastic sandals to go with the costume.

'And for me I got this:' Astrid pulled out a nun's habit.

'Way out!' Hadley said, and he fell sideways, laughing, and he had the giggles so much from the joint, he held his stomach as he laughed.

'And, because you said it's a masked ball, I got these:' Astrid rummaged about in the bead bag and took out two large Lone Ranger-type masks, and she put one to her face and gazed at Hadley as he laughed uncontrollably.

When the laughter eventually subsided, he turned off

the record player and Astrid knelt in front of him and he kissed her and stroked her hair. 'You remind me a bit of Juliet Harmer,' he whispered.

'Who?' Astrid asked, all at sea.

'She's an actress,' Hadley said with mild annoyance in his eyes as if he thought she should have known that. 'And a very pretty one at that. Haven't you ever seen *Adam Adamant*?'

'Oh yeah, I know her now,' Astrid recalled the actress now from the television, 'yeah, thanks.'

'About time we got out and about,' Hadley stood up and stretched in front of the window; a woman of about fifty was looking over at him from the top-floor window across the street. 'Nosey cow,' he murmured, 'who the He'll is she looking at?'

'Hadley!' Astrid dashed over to the switch and killed the lights, but the soft orange glow of the electric fire threw up odd shadows from Hadley's kneecaps, genitals and nipples.

'Oh, there she goes,' Hadley said with a mischievous grin, 'she's drawn the curtains!'

'We're not supposed to be here, remember,' Astrid reminded her doped boyfriend. 'They're real nosy parkers round here too. I'll get some curtain soon, no matter what you say.'

'Ah, she was just getting an eyeful,' Hadley speculated, 'probably because her fellah hasn't shagged her since the Festival of Britain.'

The light went out in the window opposite and then the curtains opened an inch.

Hadley squinted his dark-brown eyes as he looked through the window and through the sleet which seemed to be falling strangely (because of the effect of the marijuana) at the twitching curtain. 'Look at her! Thinks we can't see her; typical sex-starved middle-class voyeur – '

Astrid gathered the indigo sheet from the mattress in the corner, and to the window she dragged a straight-backed chair (which was still tacky to the touch thanks to Hadley painting it with white gloss yesterday). She stood on the chair without any offer of help from her boyfriend, and she gritted her perfect teeth as she impaled the top corners of the sheet onto two old curtain hooks. 'There,' she said angrily, 'our privacy problems solved. Now get washed and dressed.'

'Okay mother,' he said, and then he looked at the joint in the ashtray on the floor and saw that it had gone out.

'Now, Hadley!'

'Alright, don't be a fascist, child,' was his half-hearted retort, and he went to the bathroom for a quick cold shower and a painful prickly shave.

They were soon on the fogbound streets in their costumes, and masked too, making their way to the Christmas fancy dress ball held at Avalonia, the mansion of Judith Bach, self-proclaimed white witch, budding pop chanteuse, and the thrower of legendary parties and orgies. She was the daughter of a prominent surgeon with aristocratic connections. The Friday evening party would hopefully last into the early hours of a Monday morning like the last three-nighter.

On Napier Road, a Mini crawled past Hadley and Astrid – then reversed. A young man who reminded Astrid of Bob Dylan leaned over to the passenger-side window and wound it down. It was Patrick, a former art school friend of Hadley until the big fall out last year when Hadley stashed LSD at Patrick's home after calling under the pretence of a social visit. The police then raided the place and Patrick's ill mother had a seizure.

'You two aren't going to the white witch's party, are you?' Patrick queried with a lopsided grin. His pallid face looked even more ghostly in the fog.

'How did you know it was us?" Astrid lifted her mask to her forehead and shot an inane grin.

'I'd know your shape anywhere, love,' Patrick told her. 'Judith's old man crashed his Rolls. He was pissed as usual, and Judith's cancelled the do for now; its a drag.'

'Oh, well we'll go anyway,' Hadley said, and he squeezed Astrid's hand; this was their secret sign for alerting one another to a perceived lie from whoever they were talking to at the time. Astrid got the message, but wondered why Patrick would lie – unless he didn't want Hadley there for some ulterior reason.

'You'll be wasting your time, mate,' Patrick began to wind down the window.

'Can you give us a lift there?' Astrid asked, replacing the mask and leaning down to the Mini's nearside window.

'I'm not going there, love,' Patrick said, annoyed at not being believed. 'Just told you the Christmas do has been scrapped.'

'Yeah but – ' Astrid was saying when he moved off slowly down the road. The Mini melted into the fog.

'That bastard thinks I'm as daft as he is,' said Hadley.

'Maybe she *has* cancelled,' Astrid started to have doubts about Hadley's paranoid version of events.

Hadley's pace picked up and he pulled the nun

along. 'No, Judith Bach would not cancel a party if her old man jumped off Tower Bridge, and her dad's such a heathen he'd tell her to have a knees-up from his hospital bed, believe me.'

And so the couple ghosted into the London night vapours and traversed dreamlike thoroughfares were rows of owl-eyed headlights of gridlocked cars lingered with thrumming engines in the omniscient fog, and eventually they came to the leafy avenues somewhere near Kensington Gardens. Hadley seemed lost.

'Is that it over there?' Astrid pointed to a Gothic mansion with a tower, gently silhouetted in the fog.

'No, it's definitely near here, though,' Hadley assured his girlfriend.

'What's the place called again?' Astrid asked him.

'Er, Avalonia.'

Astrid looked at the wooden plaques on the gates of every million pound house she passed; all of these pretentious and puerile names engraved into them made her cringe: *Utopia, Woodlands, The Laurels, Windermere, Elfholme*... but no Avalonia.

They both heard the faint strains of music somewhere in the fog-enshrouded distance.

'The Byrds,' Astrid said, tugging the wimple from the side of her head so she could hear a little better.

'Cancelled the do my arse,' Hadley gave a type of bitter smirk and his nostrils flared. 'What a lying bastard he is.'

They walked on, and came to a dead-end.

'A cul-de-sac,' sighed Astrid, 'have you lost your bearings again?'

'It's the damned fog,' Hadley complained, 'but the music will guide us.'

The music had stopped, and a deathly silence had descended on the murky neighbourhood.

After about ten minutes of traipsing about in the limbo of mists, the fog seemed to invade Hadley's brain, obscuring his memory and sense of time and direction. And then he noticed a gilded weather cock with Father Time on, about 200 yards away – and he excitedly pointed it out to Astrid and said: 'Ah, *that* is where Avalonia lies! I knew it was somewhere in this direction.'

They came to the grand black gate pillars, and Astrid saw Judith Bach's legendary residence looming on a hill beyond the gates, at the end of a sweeping drive. Astrid expected the house to be a white stucco and pillars affair with classical decorations, but this place was the very antithesis of her expectations and looked positively sinister. It was of dark stone, originally Binny sandstone which had turned black with the grime and smoke of the centuries. The building was older than Victorian - perhaps Jacobean, and in some aspects the architecture looked almost medieval. The windows of the ground were stained glass diamond-shapes but the upper windows were burning brightly with glittering chandeliers.

Hadley grinned as he came to the front door. 'Only those who know the secret knock are admitted,' he claimed, and Astrid almost grinned.

'One-two, one-two-three, one-two-three four, Saint John!' he said with each rap of his knuckle on the hard oaken door. Footsteps echoed faintly in the hallway behind the door, and then came the rattle of a catch. The door opened and a man stood there, dressed as a butler with a hammer-tail coat.

Hadley had put his monk's hood up and he bowed and pressed his palms together, and Astrid also bowed and followed her boyfriend into the grand dwelling. The atmosphere was incredible within. Judith had apparently added gaslights to provide the illumination in the hallway, but that was nothing compared to the great oak-panelled hall. The hubbub of the chattering guests grew somewhat louder as Hadley and Astrid made their entrance. The crystal chandeliers were aglow with tiny white gas flames hissing faintly, and a huge fireplace with a mantelpiece six feet from the hearthstone was resplendent with holly and ivy and arrayed with red twisted candles. Dominating the centre of the hall was a massive circular table to rival that of King Arthur's, and seated around it were some thirty or more guests, all wearing similar fanciful robes, and this really tickled Hadley. 'Looks like we all had the same idea,' he whispered to Astrid, and had to stifle a laugh by coughing into his hand. At least he and Astrid were the only ones wearing masks. The butler escorted the couple to their places at the table, which was laid in crisp white linen, and upon it there were gleaming silver candelabra, course upon course of cutlery, elaborately-folded damask napkins containing bread rolls, ruby-studded goblets and silver buckets of champagne. In the middle of the table there stood a porcelain epergne – a type of bowl with some peculiar dark orchids and tangerines within it. Next to this the blackened metal handle of a massive ladle protruded from what looked like a cauldron which Hadley presumed to contain a punch. Hadley sat there, waiting for Judith to come in, presumably to be seated at the tall vacant black chair which seemed to represent the head of this table.

A thin tall figure in a black hooded robe, similar to that worn by Hadley, entered, and everyone stopped chattering. His hood, unlike that worn by Hadley, was very pointed, and Hadley had to laugh out loud this time because the monk in black wore a black mask too – not like his Lone Ranger styled one – but a mask all the same in the form of a black oval which covered the face. In Hadley's mind this person entering in such a dramatic slow-footed manner *had* to be Judith arsing about.

No, this person spoke, and although it was a rather effeminate high-pitched voice, it was not the sensual low voice of Judith Bach, and he seemed to say something in Latin, and suddenly, everyone stood up – and so, a sniggering Hadley rose also, a little slower than Astrid, who sensed that this was the wrong party they had somehow been admitted to.

Everyone present shouted some phrase in Latin followed by a word that sounded just like the F word. It was bizarre yet so amusing to Hadley.

'And always shall be!' said the black monk with the unmanly voice, before taking off his mask and throwing back his pointed hood. He had white swept-back hair, an exceedingly pointed chin, a long aquiline nose, and contrasting against his pallid, almost chalk-white face, were the most evil dark-ringed eyes Hadley and Astrid had ever seen. They twinkled in the light of the chandeliers and radiated pure menace, as did his wide grin. His lips looked crimson, as if he was wearing lipstick. The butler who had admitted Hadley and Astrid reappeared with a younger, similarly attired man, and the two of them were pushing a trolley upon which a silver dome rested. It seemed to be a covered dish, and it was brought to the table. The two servants struggled with this domed cover as they laboured to slide it onto the tabletop, but they managed to push it in front of the pointy-chinned head of the table. The servants then left with the trolley as the pale-faced grinning man ran a knife that was long enough to almost qualify as a sword against a sharpening rod. The butler and his assistant then returned less than a minute later with a trolley, much lighter than the previous one, and from it they took a massive Christmas pudding (which was alight with small blue flames), several fruitcakes as large and thick as car tyres topped with thick white icing and a sprig of holly.

Astrid tugged the wide sleeve of Hadley's costume and whispered: 'I think we have gate-crashed someone's party. Let's split!'

'Cool it, love,' Hadley replied, not even bothering to whisper. He expected Judith Bach to appear any moment to end this far-out charade.

But the head of the table spoke, and again it was mostly in Latin, but this time he hesitated for a moment after his unintelligible utterance – and he contorted his face for a moment, then loudly broke wind. All of the guests – except Hadley and Astrid, then cheered and swore, and threw off their hoods. Hadley didn't know any of them. They were all strangers. Two of these guests helped the head of the table to remove the domed cover, and Astrid almost fainted. It looked like a headless baby ringed with roast potatoes and green leaves of some sort.

Hadley swore, got unsteadily to his feet, but then through delayed reflexes, he recoiled with such force, the legs of his chair screeched against the wooden floor and it tipped over. The man with the weird white grinning face was not grinning now, for he was looking directly at Hadley and Astrid as he was poised to make the first cut, but he was hesitating because he was rapidly realising that there were interlopers present at this barbaric and Satanic feast!

Astrid got to her feet, and Hadley grabbed a steak-knife and almost fell over his toppled chair. The couple fled across the room from the Christmas Cannibals and Hadley yanked the door open. Astrid darted out into the hallway and upon reaching the front door she found the bolt too stiff to pull back. Hadley couldn't shift it either, and as some of the evil flesh-eating guests came into the hallway, Hadley used the blade of his knife to get some leverage against the handle of the bolt, and when a grabbing hand was a few feet away, the door was thrown open and the two young terrified gatecrashers fled down the path. Astrid reached the black wrought-iron gate first and pulled it open and she ran off blindly into the fog, crying and hardly able to breathe. Hadley ran into her back and pushed her so hard she almost fell over. He swore loudly and told her to run.

Behind them in the fog the couple heard the mass footfall of what seemed like half of the guests, and as Astrid reached a corner, she managed to let out a scream, but still she ran, and she had to lift up the habit in case it tripped her. Hadley continued to swear out of pure fear, and he gripped the handle of the steak knife hard, and knew he would have no qualms about using it if he had to.

'They've gone!' he suddenly shouted to Astrid, and

he slowed down and looked back down the dark foggy street.

Astrid continued to run off, and now she was in tears.

'Astrid! It's okay they've given up,' Hadley cried after her, panting, with a stitch in his side, but his girlfriend was so afraid she refused to slow down.

They went to a police station and told a copper what had happened, and the desk sergeant cast a sceptical eye over the two visitors dressed in their peculiar costumes.

'A baby with no head?' the sergeant asked again, leaning on the counter, pinching his eyebrow between finger and thumb.

'On a plate!' added Astrid, and she wiped tears from her eyes with the sleeve of her habit.

'And the fellah who was going to carve the baby up looked like the Joker out the *Batman* series on the telly?' The sergeant replied, revising his mental notes of Hadley's incoherent claims.

'Exactly like him - Cesar Romero – ' Hadley replied, nodding, looking at the log book on the counter, as if he expected the sergeant to write these details down.'

'Have either of you ever taken drugs?' the desk sergeant suddenly asked.

There was a guilty reaction in the eyes of Hadley Hampton-Pole, and he averted his gaze, looking down at the counter. 'No not really, man, I mean everyone has a little tote, but – '

'A little tote?' the sergeant's fierce steel-blue eyes drilled into Hadley's eyes, and he warned: 'If you are saying you use cannabis, son, then I could nick you under the Dangerous Drugs Act, 1965, and the maximum punishment for having a tote is ten years in jail and a fine for a thousand quid.'

'I don't take drugs,' Astrid said proudly, 'and I will swear on a stack of Bible's that I saw a group of Satanists or something tonight, and they had the body of a baby on a platter.'

'You won't have to swear on a stack of Bibles, love,' said the desk sergeant, 'just one will do, in a court of law, and before we get to that stage, we'll have turned your place over – just in case you two *are* doing drugs. So do you catch my drift, kids?'

There was no verbal response from Hadley or Astrid.

'So, give me your name and address, mate,' the desk sergeant asked, his pen poised over a fresh page of the log book.

'I might have been, erm, mistaken,' Hadley said in a broken voice, while in his hand he felt the steak knife handle. He was stuck between the devil and the deep blue sea. He couldn't go any further without landing himself in the shit.

'Yeah, I thought that too,' the policeman said, slowly closing the book. He depressed the silver push button on his biro. 'Night folks,' He said to their backs as the couple left.

Outside on the street, within the glow of the blue lamp, Hadley suddenly exclaimed: 'Jesus!'

Astrid jumped, startled, and asked what the matter was.

'The knife just vanished from my hand!' Hadley looked at his open palm, and Astrid could see the faint imprint of the handle of the steak knife.

They both looked down at the wet pavement – but

there was no knife to be seen there.

When they got home they sat gazing into the bars of the electric fire, and each took turns to discuss every detail of that strange night, from the time when they saw Patrick in his Mini, to the moment when they realised they were no longer being chased. And when they finally slept, Astrid kept waking with a jolt as she saw the grinning face of that man who sat at the head of the round table.

About a week after Christmas, Hadley and Astrid bumped into Judith Bach on Oxford Street, and the couple took turns in interrupting each other as they gave a garbled version of the strange Christmas fancy dress ball that had taken place on Friday 22 December.

Judith thought they were just trying to spook her at first, and said that she had not been at her home on that night, but at her father's bedside as he recovered from his crash in hospital. Hadley asked her if perhaps she had a grandfather who looked like the actor Cesar Romero, the man who played the Joker in the *Batman* TV series, but Judith said her grandfather had never lived in that house. The house she lived in had been empty for years when her father had purchased it for her, which only deepened the mystery. Furthermore, Judith said she had certainly not installed gaslights in her home and did not possess a huge round table. She invited Hadley and Astrid over to see for themselves but Astrid refused to set foot in that house. Hadley visited the mansion and saw that the hall had no chandeliers and seemed smaller than the room he had visited. 'Who were those men, then?' Hadley kept asking under his breath as he paced the hall.

'Ghosts,' Judith finally replied, and she felt a cold

sensation course down her spine.

I researched the history of the house and expected to perhaps find that some previous occupant of the gothic mansion had been an occultist, but instead my researches drew a blank. All the same, the house in question is still standing and I have heard that it has lain empty for six years and has a reputation for being haunted…

THE SINGERS

An old superstition says that to tell a lie on Christmas Eve is to court immense bad luck – and even death. Of course, there are many other superstitions associated with the same date; oxen were thought to kneel in their stalls at midnight, and young women were allowed to practice love divination rituals after sunset on Christmas Eve to see if they could ascertain the identities of their future husbands. In my many years as an investigator of the occult, I have witnessed many strange incidents on the night before Christmas, and I have also unearthed many strange tales of Christmas Eve – and here's just one of them.

In the 1980s, a 38-year-old Swindon man named Gavin started work at a printing firm in King's Lynn, Norfolk, and after living with his brother-in-law for a few months, he moved into a house on St Nicholas Street, about twenty minutes from his workplace, and although the rent was very high, Gavin paid it, and told his workmates that he had actually purchased the house outright. Gavin was always telling lies of this sort for some reason – making out he had a lot of money behind him and that he was even a distant relative to the Royal Family. Despite being a pathological liar, a girl in his office named Kimberley found herself attracted to him. She told her best friend Joanne that she liked tall men, and Gavin was 6ft 4.

Gavin played hard to get initially, and thought Kim was just after him because of his supposed wealth, but eventually, after going out on several dates with her, he realised she was not a gold digger at all, because she had actually insisted on paying for many of the meals they had at some very upmarket restaurants. And of course, Gavin - who was skinning himself to pay sky-high rent and shelling out for tailored suits to create the impression he was well-off – was only too happy to let Kimberley pay her way. This gives you some idea of how despicable Gavin was. Gavin also kept Kimberley at arm's length when she began to hint that they were virtually boyfriend and girlfriend, and whenever she vaguely suggested taking the relationship a step further, Gavin would say, 'Now, now, Kimberley, let's not get ahead of ourselves and rush into anything.'

As Christmas approached, the office workers at the printer's talked of their holiday plans, and a graphic designer of about 25 named Jeff said he was looking forward to a skiing holiday in Switzerland. Gavin suddenly said he was 'jetting to the Continent' himself for the Christmas holiday, and Kimberley, who was developing a heavy cold at the time, seemed startled by this bit of news. 'Oh, it's alright for some, isn't it?' she said, but deep down her heart was breaking because she thought he might have asked her to come with him.

'And where on the Continent are you jetting off to, old Gav?' Jeff asked, and smirked at two female co-workers, as they all suspected that Gavin was just full of bull.

'I haven't really decided yet,' Gavin replied, 'but look

out for me on the piste Jeffrey, because I might turn up in your neck of the woods.'

'Aren't you taking Kimberley with you?' Jeff asked the office fibber.

'I would but I don't think she's in any fit state to travel to snowy mountain-tops with that cold,' said Gavin, and he feigned sympathy as he looked at a sniffling Kimberley inserting a carbon into her electric typewriter.

'They say the clean air's good for colds though,' Kimberley said in a very noticeable nasal tone.

'Old wives tale,' Gavin retorted, 'and I wouldn't be surprised if that cold turns into flu. You should really be in bed.'

'You'll have to send us a few postcards from whatever exotic destination you jet off to, Gav.' Jeff suggested with a very cynical look.

'I might, if I think on,' said Gavin and inwardly cursed him.

On the following day, which was Saturday, Gavin went to do a bit of research at the local travel agent. He picked up a few Winter Holidays brochures and went home to decide on which holiday he wasn't going to take. By Monday morning back at the office, Gavin was ready for the predictable query from Jeff, and as soon as he came through the door, Jeff asked: 'Decided where you're going on your hols yet?'

'Oh, yeah, yeah,' Gavin replied, unwinding his long woollen scarf. 'I've opted for just a short break – just a week – at Andorra.'

'Very nice,' Jeff said, and he pursed his lips as if he was stifling a laugh. 'Skiing then, eh?'

Yup,' Gavin took off his jacket and hung it on the

vintage hat and coat stand he'd placed in his work area of the office.

Jeff went into the technicalities of skiing, trying to catch Gavin out, but the latter became irritated by his indirect interrogation.

'Look, Jeffrey, with all due respect, can you please stop all this?' Gavin asked him, visibly annoyed.

A silence fell as all of the office workers froze at the outburst.

'Stop all what?'

'I mean it mightn't be childish to you, Jeff, because you're what – twenty-one?'

'Twenty five.'

'Yes, well I'm nearly forty and it grates - and it seems rather infantile to me, trying to catch me out.' Gavin then stormed off to the coffee machine.

'Who got out of bed the wrong side this morning then?' Jeff asked with a smirk, and he and two of the co-workers sniggered.

They later had a minor Christmas party at the office, just a tray of mince pies, a box of Quality Street for each person from the boss, and a single bottle of Harvey's Bristol Cream, served in plastic cups to the bemused staff. Kimberley kissed Gavin under the sprig of mistletoe someone had hung from the door-closer mechanism, and Gavin reacted as if Kimberley had the bubonic plague, rubbing his mouth with his handkerchief.

'Well, see you all in a week,' Jeff said after the 'festivities' - leaving the office first, and as he was departing through the doorway he said to Gavin, 'Don't you forget that postcard now! Catch you later!'

When Gavin got home, he went into the kitchen and

looked at the cupboard stockpiled with cans of beans and packets of Vesta beef, curry and rice. The fridge-freezer was crammed with cans of lager and Guinness, Wall's Cornettos, half a dozen bottles of milk, sausages, bacon, everything he needed to sustain while he sat tight in the house for a week. The television had been moved upstairs to the bedroom, just in case someone saw the light of its cathode ray tube through the drawn curtains. Gavin would have to tiptoe about and hope that the pipes didn't make any noises when he got a wash. There was nothing he could do about the damned gurgling sound the plughole made when it was guzzling down the bathwater – but he'd just have to keep the bathroom door closed, or maybe not even bath for a week – it'd be worth it just to get one over on that irritating know-all of an arsehole Jeff.

Gavin went to the curtains on the afternoon of Christmas Eve – the day he was supposedly flying off to the wintry delights of Andorra. He moved the heavy dark green curtain aside about a centimetre and peeped out at the grey street. Could Jeff be out there, sitting in his car, trying to catch him out? Or was he being paranoid? There was no telling with Jeff; what an achievement it'd be for him to catch Gavin out and expose him to everyone in the office as an utter liar.

Gavin grabbed a choc ice and a can of lager and crept up the stairs to his bedroom. He switched on the television and turned the volume down to a whisper. What was on to make the day fly over? *The Cruel Sea* with Jack Hawkins – what a load of boring crap. Typical Christmas telly, Gavin thought. Surely there'd be something better on BBC2? Gavin gently pressed the long cylindrical button – the second one down in a row of four. A documentary about Shetland otters. Channel Four would have something new and interesting on – surely? Gavin pressed the fourth button. What was this rubbish now? He went downstairs and got the *Radio Times* and *TV Times* from the coffee table, and as he was coming through the hallway, the letterbox opened. Gavin froze.

The elderly neighbour, Mrs Johnson, had posted a Christmas card to the newcomer of St Nicholas Street, it transpired.

Gavin went upstairs and looked through the telly guide. The Channel Four programme he had on was about a Spanish 18th century monk and the cantatas he'd composed. Gavin swore under his breath. What was on ITV? The last quarter of an hour of the irritating American series *Scarecrow and Mrs King*. This was beyond boring.

The telephone started ringing downstairs.

'What the – ' Gavin got up off the bed and wondered if he should answer it. Perhaps it was his sister Jane, phoning from Manchester from some pub. She did that most Christmases – but say it was Jeff trying to catch him out? Perhaps it was Kimberley; she was forgetful at the best of times and now with that bad cold she might be ringing to have a romantic chat, not realising he was on his way to Andorra. It was odd, but Gavin had a weird, cold feeling about the caller.

He sat tight. The phone stopped ringing. He switched on the bedside radio and listened to Radio 1 on his headphones – but was that wise? Say someone decided to break in, thinking he had gone away – he wouldn't hear them with those headphones – so Gavin unplugged them and turned the volume down to barely audible level. He went back downstairs and grabbed a bundle of paperbacks, and then, as he passed the kitchen, he nipped in quickly, opened the fridge, and took out two cans of lager.

He dozed off reading a book, and woke with a headache about 7pm. The room was in darkness except for the glowing green digital readout of his bedside alarm clock. He made sure the thick curtains were drawn and then he clicked on the bedside lamp. He felt hungry, so he went down to the kitchen, taking care to avoid the creaky spots on the landing. In the kitchen he sliced the red cheese and chopped half an onion to put in the Breville sandwich toaster. He had another can of lager as he waited for the toaster. He was that preoccupied with various imagined scenarios where Jeff found him out, he ended up biting into the sealed toasted sandwich and burning his lip and tongue on molten cheddar. He gulped down the icy lager to sooth the injuries. He went back to bed and wondered if he could live like this for a week. Perhaps he could say that the plane had developed engine trouble and he'd had to come home?

His own snoring woke him around midnight and he could hardly swallow because his uvula had swollen up because of the loud snores. He went to the bathroom, looked at his face in the shaving mirror on the ledge over the wash basin, and then cupped his hand under the running cold water tap. He gently threw the water in his hands into his face and grimaced. Then he snatched the soft towel from the chrome pole and buried his puffed-up face in it as he exhaled.

It was then when he thought he heard the carollers.

He turned off the tap and listened. The singing

sound was fainter now.

He went back into the bedroom and looked at the bedside clock again. It really was past midnight – so what were carol singers doing out at this time? It was Christmas now, he realised, and explained the singing away by imagining it was probably the sound of a hymn being sung at the midnight Christmas mass at the nearby Chapel of St Nicholas.

But the sounds of the singers were heard again – and they sounded much nearer – at two in the morning. This time he went to the window, and believing it was safe to look out at such an unearthly hour, he parted the curtains and opened the window. No, the sounds were not coming from out there – so *where* were they coming from?

At this point, Gavin noticed the goosebumps rising up on his forearms. 'Oh come on, man' he said to himself with a forced grin, 'don't start all that spooky crap.'

He sat up on the bed, and browsed through the *Radio Times* when all of a sudden, there came a loud burst of singing to his left. His first, immediate thought was that someone had somehow gained entry to the house. Out the left corner of his eye, Gavin saw something black emerge, and his heart pounded with fear as he turned left to see what it was. It was someone in a long black robe, similar to the habit a nun wears, but instead of seeing a face in profile within the hood, he saw the nose-less profile of a skull! This terrifying apparition would have been enough to stop the heart of even the most sceptical person at that time in the morning, but there was another identically robed skeletal being behind her, and another behind that one too – and they were carrying a coffin. The train of these solid-looking ghosts in black moved slowly out of the wall, and there were eight of them in all, four on either side of the coffin. They were singing at the top of their voices but Gavin could not understand a word of their strange song. It seemed to be Latin. Gavin came out with a string of profanities because of his shattered nerves, and the ghostly pallbearers in black halted – and slowly they oriented themselves so that the front end of the coffin was pointing at him.

The nightmarish skeletal women then opened their jawbones wide and out came the words: 'She's dead! She's dead!' And then they said some other unintelligible word and went up slowly in pitch to a shriek, and as they did this, the four pallbearers at the front lowered themselves, tilting the coffin towards Gavin, who was frozen in terror. He could see that the lid was not on that coffin, and there was a body in a white shroud within it, and the person in it looked as pale as the shroud it was wrapped in, and then suddenly he recognised the dead person. It was Kimberley.

'She's dead!' the pallbearers all shrieked in unison, and then the four at the front straightened up and they all laughed as they turned left by almost ninety degrees. They then continued on their way – and walked in a grim procession into the solid wall. Just before Gavin cried out and bolted from the room, he saw the black trailing cloth of the last pallbearer's robe going through the skirting board.

Gavin almost fell down the stairs in the dark, and upon reaching the hallway, he turned on the light and went straight to the door. He unbolted it and ran out into the freezing street. He went to Mrs Johnson's house and hammered on the door as he looked up at his bedroom window, trying to estimate the point in the wall next to the curtained window where those eight evil ghosts had emerged. Eventually, the letterbox of the elderly neighbour opened and Mrs Johnson's bloodshot eyes met Gavin's bulging and frightened eyes.

'Who is it?' Mrs Johnson asked with a tremor in her weak voice.

'It's me, Gavin, from next door, Mrs Johnson! Can you open the door please?'

'Yes, wait there,' she said, and then as the letterbox closed and she went further into the house to get the keys her voice faded to a whisper.

She opened the door minutes later and Gavin felt so stupid when she asked him what the matter was.

'Mrs Johnson, you won't believe this, but eight ghosts walked through my bedroom just now!'

'You'd better come in,' she said, and as she yelped in shock as her cat, Toby saw the opportunity to rush into the house after being out all day, Gavin also yelped, as his nerves had been frayed by the recent encounter with the supernatural beings.

Mrs Johnson lit the gas fire and put the kettle on, and she said something which astounded Gavin. 'Where they all in black?' she said, with a curious knowing look in her red and weary eyes.

'Yes! Eight of them, and they were carrying a – a –'

'A coffin? Oh dear.' Mrs Johnson went into the kitchen and came back to put two china cups and their saucers on the table.

'How did you *know?*' Gavin held his palms out to the

gas fire and those hands were shaking.

'I saw them once,' Mrs Johnson revealed. 'The singers, they call them.'

'What are they?' Gavin asked, and his throat felt like sandpaper.

'I don't know, but it's very bad to see them,' Mrs Johnson told him, and looked into the blue and white flames of the gas jets.

'They showed me the body of a girl – my girlfriend – in a coffin,' Gavin told his neighbour and his whole body shook as he relived the incident in describing it.

'Oh dear,' Mrs Johnson said, 'I'm so sorry.'

'Do you think it's been a warning?' Gavin wondered out loud.

'Too late for a warning, I'm afraid,' Mrs Johnson said, and the kettle started to whistle.

Later that day, Gavin abandoned his ridiculous charade and he went to the house where Kimberley lived, and when her father opened the door, Gavin saw that he had red eyes. He'd been crying. Her father seemed hollow, somehow, as if he was just a shell.

'Kimberley's dead,' he told Gavin, and seemed to look through him. But then he stepped aside. 'We phoned you but you must have been out.'

Gavin recalled the telephone call he never answered at his home. 'What happened?' he asked, and went into the house where he saw Kimberley's mother lying on the sofa, surrounded by people he had never set eyes on before; probably relatives and friends who had come to comfort the lady. Gavin was told that Kimberley's cold had rapidly turned into a bad case of pneumonia and that deceptive respiratory disease had claimed her life. It was a fairly commonplace occurrence, Gavin later learned from his own doctor.

What made it even more tragic was Gavin's realisation that he had loved Kimberley – and yet he had not really known it when she was alive. Now he felt a great sense of loss, and he hated himself because of the way he had been so stand-offish towards her. He realised that he should have been going abroad for real – with Kimberley. Gavin was so upset by what he saw as the lost love of Kimberley, he gave up his job and went home to Manchester.

From what I have gathered over the years, the "singers" – as Mrs Johnson calls the phantom pallbearers – are not confined to Norfolk. Very similar coffin-carrying figures in black have been reported to me from Glastonbury, Bath, Hull, Newcastle, Liverpool, and also Edinburgh. They seem to be some sort of banshee, and they are most active in the winter for some unknown reason. Keep *your* ears peeled for them this winter...

TRUTH BE TOLD

In December 1982 a thick fog covered the north west of England and a woman in her fifties named Claire went to visit the grave of her mother in a certain Cheshire churchyard. Claire worked in the Vauxhall car plant as a secretary and was a very level-headed lady who had no belief or interest in the paranormal. The fog was becoming that thick she could hardly see objects more than six feet away. Claire put an ornamental vase containing poinsettia flowers on her mother's grave and looked at the inscription, and she thought she'd gone to the wrong grave at first, for instead of:

In Loving Memory of
Mother
Quietly remembered every day
Always in Our Hearts

The inscription read:

Here lies a selfish mouldy cow
Six feet in the earth below
She only loved herself and money
She rots below where it's never sunny

Claire felt dizzy with shock when she saw these golden letters inscribed upon the black marble headstone. She adjusted her spectacles, glanced at the name at the top of the gravestone, and saw it was indeed her mother Elizabeth's name there, but who had put this wicked inscription on it? Claire rifled through her handbag for her inhaler, for she felt an asthma attack coming on, she was that wound up by this sick practical joke. But how would a prankster erase the verse that had been inscribed there and replace it with this sinister one? She felt this was more than some earthly black joke – that something supernatural was behind it, and with this uncanny suspicion in her mind and the gathering gloom of the late afternoon and the wreathing, sodden fog, she thought she should get out of that place of the dead as soon as possible. She looked behind her, because Claire felt as if the depraved author of this shocking desecration was lurking nearby in the swirling mist, enjoying her reaction to his unholy verse. She stumbled away from the grave and looked about. There was not another soul in that cemetery, and yet Claire felt she was being watched. She happened to look towards the white marble headstone of another grave, and although it was a grave she hadn't really noticed before, the inscription on it gave her quite a jolt:

One Stupid Bastard Lies Here
He drove a car while full of beer
Killed himself and a little child
And burns in Hell for three pints of mild

Claire read this horrible inscription and hurried towards the gates of the cemetery, and on the way she caught glimpses of many other strange verses on the headstones, and she slowly realised that whatever was responsible for this unearthly form of vandalism had not only ruined her mother's gravestone, but many others as well. As she dashed through the gateway, Claire thought she heard a man's laughter somewhere, but she didn't turn around. She got into her car, and as she drove off she felt tears streaming from her eyes. She thought about that weird inscription that had appeared on her mum's headstone and knew deep down that her late mother *had* undoubtedly been rather vain about her looks, and, come to think of it, she *had* been obsessed with money – but who, beyond the family and a close circle of friends, would have known about those flaws in her mother? And who on earth would go to the trouble of inscribing her deceased mother's faults on a gravestone? Even in the car with the cemetery behind her now barely visible in the rear-view mirror, Claire had the unsettling impression that something had followed her into the car from the graveyard, but it was probably just her imagination, heightened by the very strange incident which had just taken place.

When she arrived home, Claire told her husband Peter about the shocking inscriptions on her mother's gravestone and the other headstones and Peter said that it would be impossible for any practical joker to put gold lettering on the black marble of the headstone of her mother – or any other headstone for that matter, unless it had simply been some plate of black plastic that had been stuck over the original inscription – but Claire dismissed this possibility, for she had plainly seen that the upsetting verse had been engraved into the marble, and whoever or whatever was responsible for this diabolical work had done the same on the other gravestones.

Peter promised he'd stop off at the cemetery in the morning on his way to work and have a look for himself, and this he did. It was his last day at work before the Christmas break and there was a sparkling frost on the path of the cemetery as Peter walked along in the rays of the rising sun, eyeing the various headstones. He saw nothing out of the ordinary, just the usual 'In Loving Memory' and ' RIP' inscriptions. At last he reached the black marble headstone of his mother in law, and it said nothing about a 'selfish mouldy cow' – just the familiar inscription about being 'quietly remembered every day'. Peter immediately turned and left the cemetery and got into his car. As he drove for his workplace – a factory at Ellesmere Port, he wondered if his wife had been seeing things, and if so, was this some symptom of an approaching nervous breakdown?

On Christmas Eve, Peter and Claire went to one of the oldest pubs in Chester, the Old Boot Inn, an atmospheric low-beamed premises which dates back to the 17th century, and there the couple got talking to an old Irishman named Noel who had lived in Cheshire for about thirty years, and during a conversation with Noel, his glass was seen to move slightly of its own accord on the bar counter. Noel joked that the glass had been nudged by the ghost that was reputed to haunt the Old Boot, and so the course of the conversation turned to the supernatural. Claire suddenly recalled the spooky inscriptions in the cemetery, and she said to Peter, 'Shall I tell Noel about those weird horrible verses that appeared on the gravestones?'

'Oh, don't bring all *that* up, love,' Peter advised her, because he thought Noel would think his wife was nuts, and he held her hand and gave two little squeezes as a signal for her to say nothing more - but Noel's eyes suddenly widened, and the old man said: 'Ah, wait a minute, I think I know what you're going to tell me,' and he named the very cemetery (which was nowhere near Chester) where Claire's mother had been buried, and then he told the couple something very odd. 'I know someone, a good lad from Liverpool named Danny who has three members of his family interred there,' Noel said with a very earnest expression and a furrowed brow, 'and he saw the inscription change on a tomb there. The words and that actually changed before his eyes, and I think it was the tomb of some big major or captain in the military, but anyway, the language – I wouldn't repeat what it said in front of a lady – '

Claire's eyes widened behind her spectacles, and then she looked at Peter, who had taken a sharp inhalation from his cheroot as he squeezed his wife's hand. 'No, please do,' Claire urged the Irishman, 'was it something rude?'

'Claire…' Peter said to her and blue smoke came out of his mouth as he spoke her name.

'Well I won't embarrass or offend you or your husband Claire, but the words on the tomb were foul; absolutely obscene, and then Danny saw that the same thing had happened with the inscriptions on the other gravestones, but the one on his family's grave hadn't changed for some reason. Well, Danny was out of there like a shot, and he was later told by some of the locals that the verses on the graves did that now and then, always around Christmas, and no one knows why or what's behind it, but I think it's the other fellah below.'

Claire went cold inside when Noel told her this, and what the Irishman said is supposedly true, for I have researched the cemetery story for years and the tale of the changing inscriptions goes back well over a hundred years, and I believe something similar has been reported in other cemeteries in Lancashire, but why the phenomenon happens and who or what is behind it remains unknown. Claire stopped going to her mother's grave during the month of December after Noel vindicated her experience.

THE RED MAN

Since the UK's National Lottery started in 1993, it has given Britain over three thousand millionaires, and of course, many of these people have had their lives changed (and not always for the better) overnight by receiving such huge amounts of prize money. One Merseyside man I shall call Mike certainly had his lifestyle changed when he won around three million quid in the 1990s. Mike and his wife Gemma had always wanted to move to live in the French countryside, and this dream became a reality after Mike scooped those millions. He and Gemma and his 5-year-old son Daniel moved into a beautiful farmhouse in the Manche department in Normandy near to the commune of Villedieu-les-Poêles, and the renovated farmhouse dated back to Napoleonic times. The couple and their child moved into the farmhouse in time for Christmas, and on Christmas Eve, little Daniel went to bed around 8.15pm, and his mum Gemma could see he was very excitable, not only because of the new surroundings but because in the mind of a child, Christmas Eve really was a time when Santa was on his way and the most exciting day of the year was imminent. Gemma read Daniel a few stories and then tucked him in, and when she looked in on him at 9.30pm she saw he was sleeping soundly.

However, when Gemma and Mike retired to their bedroom just after midnight, they noticed something odd. Mike was sticking the tags on his son's gift-wrapped presents when he heard a noise. It sounded like a man's voice. Gemma noticed it around the same time as she was brushing her hair as she sat in front of a dresser. The couple looked at one another. The farmhouse was in the middle of the country and although it was fully alarmed, they both read the newspapers and watched the news programmes and were only too aware that it was always possible for professional burglars to bypass alarms.

Mike tilted his head and with a look of dread he said, 'It sounds like someone talking in Daniel's room.'

There was a sharp intake of breath from Gemma, and she got up from the chair at the dresser and she and Mike simultaneously went to the bedroom door. Mike put his forefinger to his lips, gesturing for his worried wife to be quiet, and then he sneaked along the carpeted landing and halted outside the door of Daniel's bedroom. Yes, there was definitely someone talking in there, and Mike's heart skipped a beat. He paused for a moment, and then turned the handle of the door and barged in – and there was Daniel, sitting up in his bed, and the moonlight shining into the dark room through the lattice window cast diamonds of silvery light on his son's face. Mike switched the light on and looked around as his wife came into the bedroom.

'Where is he?' he asked his son.

'He disappeared,' Daniel replied, and seemed bewildered.

The curtains covering the two windows of the room went right down to the carpet, and it was possible – but probably not that likely – that some nut could be hiding behind them. Mike swished the curtains apart just in case. There was no one there. Then he checked the two windows – and saw that the casement stays were still fastened securely and the locks were still on. As Gemma sat next to her son and hugged him, Mike checked the wardrobe – no one was there. He looked under the bed – and there was no one there, either.

'Who was he?' Gemma found herself asking her son.

'He was a man, and he was all in red,' Daniel told her, and then he asked his mum: 'Can I sleep with you and Daddy?

'Of course you can, love,' Gemma told him, and her husband sat on the bed and began to quiz the boy.

'Where did he come from, Daniel?' he asked.

Daniel shrugged.

'Did he wake you up?' Gemma asked.

Daniel nodded. 'He touched my face and I woke up.'

'What did he say?' Mike asked, still not realising that this mysterious visitor was of a supernatural origin.

'He said he was going to make me great,' was Daniel's odd reply.

'Make you great?' Gemma was baffled by her son's claim.

'You don't think this place has a secret passage do you?' Mike asked Gemma in all seriousness.

'I don't think so,' Gemma said, looking around at the old walls. 'I don't know.'

Mike went around the room, tapping on the walls with his knuckle – seeing if there were any hollow-sounding spots – and there weren't.

'Maybe he was talking in his sleep,' Gemma suggested.

'I heard that voice, and it did not sound like a 5-year-old boy,' Mike recalled the tone and accent of the eerie speaker – it had sounded like someone foreign speaking English.

The boy slept with his parents that night, and the next morning, Daniel had a great Christmas. He opened his presents and his mum videoed his reaction to all of the lovely gifts she and Mike had bought for him. Before the Lottery win, Mike had been in a low-paid job and Gemma had been on benefit because of a back injury, but now they were living their dream and Gemma felt herself becoming choked when she saw the way Daniel's face was lighting up with all the presents.

On Boxing Day, around 1pm, Gemma came out of the shower and wrapped a towel around her head as she went into the bedroom. She glanced out the window and saw Mike building a snowman for Daniel in the middle of the vast garden – and then she noticed something very sinister indeed. At the end of the garden, standing just to the left of the gate with the roof over it, there was a tall thin man, and he was dressed in vivid scarlet. Although he was about a hundred yards away, Gemma could see that he had a very pale – almost white – face, and he had on a shirt with a frilly white front. Gemma opened the window, and she saw the creepy strangely-attired man hide behind the lychgate – as if he knew she was watching him. Gemma shouted to Mike, and he and Daniel turned to face her, and as they did, the man in red moved so quickly away from the lychgate he was just a blur. He was gone in a second.

Mike shouted: 'What?'

Gemma beckoned him, but again he flicked back his head, signifying that he couldn't hear her, so – despite the freezing cold outdoors of December – Gemma put on her slippers and went outside in ankle-deep snow in her bathrobe. She told Mike about the man in red, and he went to turn to look towards the lychgate but Gemma told him not to – and pleaded for him to come inside with Daniel at once. Mike therefore abandoned the snowman and picked up Daniel to take him inside, where he stood in front of a blazing log fire.

'Who is he?' Mike mused on the enigmatic visitor haunting his new home.

'Mike, do you think he's a – ' Gemma looked down at Daniel, and, seeing he was conveniently distracted as he played with a toy tractor on the hearthrug – she whispered the rest of the sentence: ' – ghost?'

'I don't know,' Mike admitted, and he looked into the flames of the fire for a moment, then directed his gaze towards the window. 'Maybe our dream house has an unsavoury history,' he said, pensively.

Gemma went to the front door and put the bolt on.

'That won't stop him if he is a ghost,' Mike remarked and grinned.

'That's not funny,' Gemma told him, and she went to the window and looked out at the white desolation of the countryside beyond the garden. The bare branches were dusted with snow and now, showing faintly through the snow clouds, Gemma could make out the vague disc of the dying sun.

Then she saw a ruby speck, about a quarter of a mile away, next to the trunk of a tree which looked as thin as a matchstick to her.

'There he is! He's back!' she said, and turned to look at Mike, who was startled by her words.

'Who's back?' Daniel asked, looking up from the plastic yellow tractor.

Mike reached the window and looked out. 'Where?'

'See where that hill is?' Gemma pointed and the tip of her index finger touched the window pane. 'Well just to the – '

Mike interrupted her because he'd spotted him. 'I see him! Who the hell is he?'

'It's weird you know,' said Gemma, 'its as if he knows we are watching him – that's the feeling I get.'

Mike walked away from the window.

'Don't go outside!' Gemma warned.

'I'm going upstairs to get the binoculars,' Mike reassured her and he got to the stairs and he leaped up them three steps at a time. The figure was still there in the snowy distance when he returned with the 25 x 50 binoculars. Mike trained them on the rose-red spot and thumbed the focus wheel. 'He's dressed in what looks like a red velvet suit,' Mike told Gemma. 'And he has on a white shirt with all frills down the front. His hair's white, and it looks like one of those wigs that they wore in the French Revolution days.'

'Let's have a look,' Gemma asked, full of curiosity now.

Mike handed the binoculars to her.

Gemma had much superior eyesight than her husband, and she could almost see the face of the sinister man in the blood-red clothes. She could certainly see that his eyes were dark – like two black points the size of a full stop.

'Let's have another look,' Mike reached out for the binoculars.

Gemma handed the binoculars to her husband, and

then she wondered if the weird stalker was out to kidnap Daniel, perhaps to get his hands on some of the money they'd won. 'Mike, I think we should call the police. What's their number in France? 112 isn't it?'

'Don't start calling anyone just yet, he might just be a nut,' Mike said.

'Which is an even bigger reason to call the police,' Gemma said, and she picked up the telephone, ready to dial 112 – but the telephone line was dead. Gemma gulped and she pressed the hook switch a few times but still the line was silent as the grave. At that time in the 1990s, mobile phones were not as common as they are now and the couple did not own a mobile device.

'He's just vanished – right before my eyes!' Mike told Gemma, and he lowered the binoculars and looked into the distance with his naked eyes to make sure the man in the Venetian red outfit hadn't simply stepped outside the limited field of view of the binoculars. He was nowhere to be seen, and now a faint wind was howling at the windows and dislodging feathery lace-white accumulations of snow from the roof and window ledges.

'Do you think he's cut the telephone line?' Gemma asked her husband. She always relied on Mike to allay any of her worries, but he just shrugged.

'I don't think this fellah is part of some group out to kidnap anyone,' Mike replied, looking again through the binoculars. 'Maybe this thing is a *ghost*,' he said, and mindful of Daniel's presence, Mike said the word 'ghost' as softly as he could.

'So you don't think he's a criminal or anything?'

'Well, criminals generally keep a low profile,

especially would-be kidnappers,' Mike reasoned, 'they don't go round wearing red suits.'

'Santa Claus wears a red suit,' Daniel suddenly said, but Gemma put on a brave smile and told her son to play with a robot he'd received from his Nan. Daniel ran to the robot in the corner and switched it on.

'How in heaven did he get there?' Mike uttered the words in a gasp of astonishment, removing the binoculars from his eyes. He went nearer to the window. 'He's at the gate now.'

'Oh my God – what?' Gemma looked out and saw the stranger was indeed standing there. He opened the gate, and began walking towards the house along the snow-covered path. He covered about ten feet – and then halted, and turned around. And then he vanished.

'Jesus,' was all Mike could say, and Gemma started to take deep breaths, something she always did when she was in shock. Mike recalled her doing the same when the police called at her home one day and told her that her younger brother had been seriously injured in a car crash. Thankfully he recovered, but Mike recalled that gasping for air and the panic attacks it led to in the middle of the night.

The couple kept watch for about forty minutes at the window and the snow began to fall as the light of day steadily faded. The blinds were closed on all of the windows and the television was put on and turned up. There was no cable service installed at the house and no internet, and they had to watch French TV shows just in an effort to distract their mind from the ghost.

Daniel bravely told his mother he wanted to sleep in his own room tonight, even though she wanted him to sleep between her and Mike. 'I'm a big boy, mum,' he said, adding: 'Big boys don't get scared and sleep in their own room.'

By midnight, Daniel was sleeping in his room, and Gemma had left his door ajar, just in case he was visited again.

The couple sat up in bed, listening to the wind that was now wailing around the farmhouse. The snow was falling heavily, and despite Gemma's advice to keep away from the window, Mike was periodically pushing the curtain aside and looking out into the nightscape. He kept expecting the man in the red suit to be down there in the snow, but there wasn't a living soul about.

Mike tried to read a book as he sat up and Gemma looked through a clothing catalogue. The silence in the bedroom was very tense all the same, and the occasional shriek of the banshee wind did nothing to lessen the fraught atmosphere.

Mike dozed off, still sitting up with the paperback in his hands at around 2.40am, and Gemma gently took the book from his soft grasp and placed it on her bedside cabinet. She then held Mike's hand and removed one of the large pillows that had been supporting her. She lay back, and then her mind became full of all of those surreal things that flow through our consciousness when we are on the cusp of sleep.

At 4am something awoke Gemma. Her eyes took in the ceiling as she heard a voice. *That* voice again. Her heart pounded. He was next door – in Daniel's room again.

'Mike,' she whispered, and shook his arm.

Mike jolted in the bed and kicked his leg out as his eyelids flew open.

'He's back!' she said a little louder now.

Immediately, Mike got up out the bed and hurried to the doorway.

Gemma looked about for something to hit the ghost with, and then she realised how pointless it would be.

Mike reached the door of Daniel's room and saw that it was now closed. That door had been ajar at half-past three when he had gone to the toilet. Mike barged in and once again he saw Daniel sitting up. 'Was that man in red here again?'

Daniel nodded, and pointed to the curtains.

Mike looked towards the window, to the curtains that went down to the carpet – and there, protruding from the bottom of those curtains, were the red leather toecaps of a pair of rather long shoes! He was still here!

There was more anger in Mike than fear – he was absolutely livid at someone or something that was visiting his only son in the dead of night. He lunged forward and tore the curtains aside, revealing something unearthly. The man in red stood there and showed no fear on his chalk-white face, no flicker of acknowledgement in his black irises. He wore that white periwig which belonged to the 18th century, along with that white satin shirt with the ruffled front and its frilly cuffs which contrasted with the peculiar three-quarter coat of scarlet velvet.

Gemma's screams pierced the air from the doorway.

'What the hell do you want with my son?' Mike roared, and he closed his hands into hard fists and took up a stance that made it clear that he wanted to lay into this unearthly anachronistic freak.

'Do you know what you have here?' the stranger

suddenly said in a voice that did not seem to have the normal acoustical properties of a living person. There was a flatness, an unemotional quality to the timbre of the voice that really unnerved Gemma, and she rushed forward and dragged Daniel from the bed and took him into her room as she called for Mike to follow her.

But Mike stood his ground, and believed that the person standing before him was nothing like any ghost he had ever imagined. He seemed real, and liable to bleed if he was punched hard in the nose or battered with a chair – and there was a little cricket bat of Daniel's in the corner which Mike had suddenly noticed.

'That boy is very special, and he could rule the world!' the stranger said, stepping forward.

'Who are you?' Mike asked, ready to throw a punch.

'I don't think you'd even be able to take the answer in to that question,' the intruder told him, and as he smiled his face seemed contorted – like someone who'd had a little too much plastic surgery. He stopped advancing and once again asked: 'Do you know what you have in Daniel? I bet you haven't got a clue what I am even talking about.'

'Get out of here now!' Mike yelled. 'Go back to wherever you came from, and don't ever come back!'

The man shook his head. 'Your son could be great! I can make your son the ruler of this world! Do you understand that?'

'Get out of this house now you weird bastard!' Mike pulled back his fist, ready to have a go at chinning him. But suddenly the man in red was gone. Mike looked at the spot where he had stood, then thought he'd go and tell Gemma he'd sent him packing.

The most bloodcurdling scream Mike had ever heard erupted from the bedroom next door. It was the scream of his wife. His stomach then somersaulted as he heard her cry: 'Get away from him!'

Mike flew out of the room, onto the landing, and charged into his bedroom, to find Gemma with her hands on her face, looking at the backdated man in the red velvet clothes. Daniel was behind the supernatural trespasser.

'I am not going to harm Daniel!' the ghost bawled at her. 'I merely want to take him under my –'

Mike threw his right fist into the milk-white niveous face of the tangible phantom, but as his knuckle impacted into the jawbone, the figure vanished, and Mike continued forward with the raw momentum and hit the wall with such force, he almost knocked himself out.

The ghost did not return, even though the couple and their son expected it to, and they spent the remainder of that morning downstairs in the lounge with all the lights on. The harassed family found accommodation in a hotel forty miles away and with great bitterness they decided to sell the farmhouse. Mike pondered on the nature of the child-obsessed ghost in red for years, and eventually related the story to me. When I heard about the offer of the ghost to make Daniel great – and a ruler of the world, it all started to fall into place, and then of course, I remembered how the colour of the visitant's clothes also concurred with my theory. As far-fetched as I knew it would sound, I presented my conjecture to Mike and Gemma, and later backed it up with references and documents the couple could check for themselves – and they *did* check out those references too, and they eventually believed my theory. Here is what I proposed regarding the man in scarlet.

Throughout European history, a number of mysterious figures are seen to surface, vanish into obscurity for a while, only to resurface in the annals of the Continent – and Britain. We have the mysterious Count of St Germain, a man I have written quite a lot about over the years. The Count was an unfathomable person who seemed to be aristocratic, and if we take the evidence of various diarists of note in sever5al countries from the 17th century to Victorian times, we must accept that he was either immortal or someone with an abnormally long lifespan of at least 120 years – and despite being 120 he always looked like a man in his mid-forties. He is mentioned by Marie Antoinette, the French philosopher Voltaire, Horace Walpole, Clive of India Catherine the Great, and many more history-makers. The Count was said to be a successful alchemist and a supreme occultist who had possessed the Elixir of Youth and the Philosopher's Stone. Next, we come to the mysterious *Red Man* - a baffling shadowy figure who dates back even further than the Count of St Germain, and whereas the Count aroused suspicion and awe, mere mention of the Red Man would send ripples of fear throughout the superstitious societies of Europe, be it the 15th century or the 20th century. One of the earliest mentions of this mysterious man, who, as his name suggests, dressed in a red velvet suit, was around Christmas 1564, during the construction of the Tuileries - the royal and imperial palace, in France. The palace was planned by Catherine de Medici, who had been the Queen of

France from 1547 to 1559. She met the Red Man and initially taking him to be a peculiar individual, she evidently realised he was not a flesh and blood person after something happened which she never specified. She did, however, believe the encounter with him was an omen of bad luck, especially as his clothes were blood-red in colour. Catherine lived to the age of 69 though, dying in 1589, but she lived in mortal fear of encountering the Red Man again, and no one knows what he said to her or why she was so afraid of him. Some think the Red Man warned her about the St. Bartholomew's Day Massacre of 1572, in which many thousands (some say 30,000) of Huguenots were slaughtered by mobs of Catholics.

In early 1610 the Red Man was seen again, this time confronting King Henry IV of France. Not long after the meeting with the eerie crimson man of mystery, Henry IV was assassinated in Paris on 14 May of that year by a Catholic fanatic named Francoise Ravaillac, who stabbed him with a dagger.

There were more encounters with the Red Man after this in the following century, the best documented one being the day he was seen in the bedroom of the doomed French monarch King Louis XVI. At this time, the King and his Queen, Marie Antoinette, were making futile attempts at escaping the clutches of the revolutionaries by fleeing to Varennes – which would end in disaster and ultimately death, for Louis was guillotined on 21 January of the following year, and on 16 October of that year – 1793 – at fifteen minutes past noon, Marie Antoinette was also beheaded on the bladed death machine and her head and body were afterwards dumped in an unmarked grave. There were strange stories of a distinguished man in red clothes who had visited Marie Antoinette as she awaited her execution, but what his business was with the damned former monarch is unknown.

The Red Man then appeared to Napoleon Bonaparte several times in 1798, the year before he seized power and installed himself as First Consul. It is not known precisely what the Red Man said to Napoleon, but there were rumours from those closest to the future Emperor of the French that the mysterious visitor had struck a bargain with him which would put Napoleon on a path for the domination of Europe – and afterwards – the world. The Red Man had told Napoleon that he had known him since he was a boy and had known even in those early days that he had possessed a great potential for world leadership. 'I know more of your inner self, your weaknesses – which are few – and your strengths, which hold such promise,' the Red Man told Napoleon. 'I know you even more than you know yourself.'

The Red Man then visited Napoleon periodically and advised him on his many campaigns , and when Napoleon was crowned Emperor of France by Pope Pius VII on 2 December 1804, the Red Man put in an appearance later on that evening of the coronation and also at Christmas Eve. The final appearance of the Red Man in Napoleon's life was on the morning of New Year's Day, 1814, just four months before the Emperor would be forced to abdicate before being banished to the isle of Elba. On this occasion there was a level-headed witness to Napoleon's meeting with the Red Man – Count Mole, the Counsellor of State. He admitted the Red Man into Napoleon's cabinet, where the depressed military giant had shut himself away from everyone. Prompted by a burning curiosity, Mole listened at the keyhole to the conversation between Napoleon and the weird-looking man in red. He heard the Red Man telling Napoleon what to do and how he'd meet with disaster and exile if he didn't do as he was told, but of course, it all ended at Waterloo for Napoleon in 1815, but that was not the end of the Red Man. It is said by some occultists that he found another young subject in a boy named Adolf Hitler, and strangely enough, many in Hitler's inner circle spoke of having the impression that someone was behind the decisions Hitler made during his many military campaigns. Could this mystifying Red Man be the same entity – attired in outdated scarlet clothes and a white periwig - which told the 5-year-old boy Daniel that it could make him great? If it was, then has that creepy entity moved on to some other suitable young person somewhere else in the world since then? And could this child be guided by the entity to become the next Napoleon or Hitler?

CRYSTAL CLEAR

On Christmas morning, 1988, a family of six in North London were opening their presents. Cliff Richard's seasonal hit, *Mistletoe and Wine* was playing on Radio 1 on the big portable "Ghetto Blaster" stereo that 13-year-old Mike had got off his parents – Patsy and Mark, along with six other gifts ranging from a BMX Bike to a Nintendo Entertainment System. Mike's younger brother David, aged 11, was wearing his replica Ghostbusters Proton Pack as he sat playing games on the Commodore 64 he had plugged into the TV without even asking anyone if they were watching *The Pink Panther Show*. He also wore a Flik Flak Swiss Watch for Children timepiece on his wrist, one of the few gifts from his Nan he actually liked. Carly - aged 9 - had cleared the coffee table to play with two of the more interesting toys she'd received from her mum and dad this Christmas – the fold-out kingdom of Castle Lovely Locks with her 8-and-a-half inch dolls named Maidens and little animals called Pixietails. And on the same 'floor' of the coffee table, Carly had set up Sindy's Kitchen Café, which, as the name suggests, consisted of a fairly realistic mock-up set of a café's kitchen for the Sindy doll with such features as a serving hatch, dishwasher, microwave oven, fridge, drop-leaf counter and a hob. And Carly had all the accessories to go with this, including a pop-up-toaster, jug kettle, a portable TV and a wall-mounted telephone.

On the floor with his mum Patsy, 2-year-old Bernie was baffled by his main present - a Playskool Fold and Go Activity Quilt. As his mum tried to get the tot to explore the rattling and supposedly interesting colourful tactile objects, Bernie seemed more fascinated with his sister Carly's unopened presents lying next to her feet, and he tried to grab one of them – a royal blue box with silver Christmas tree patterns upon it, secured with a red satin self-adhesive bow.

'Hey! Leave that alone, Bernie!' Carly stopped playing with Sindy and took the unopened gift off him.

Bernie gave a fake cry and reached up for the ascending present with both arms.

'Look, Bernie, what's this?' his mum said, flapping the ears of a pink bunny on the Activity Mat, but Bernie grunted and made a fist at her.

The father of the family, Mark, meanwhile, was reading the listings of the *Radio Times* and tutting. He wanted to see the first showing of *Back to the Future* on BBC1 at 3.10pm, but knew David would probably still want to use the TV to play on his Commodore 64 computer. Mark considered going next door to watch the film in his neighbour Terry's house after the Christmas dinner, as his mother-in-law would no doubt turn up around then.

Carly opened the gift her baby brother had wanted, and she gave him the wrapper, which made him chuckle and kick his legs. He tasted it and put the bow in his mouth.

'Giz that, Bernie!' his mother yanked the bow out of his mouth and the little mite cried.

'Mum, what's this?' Carly asked, and read the two big bright words on the cube-shaped box, which was quite heavy: Madame Rosa. The Box depicted a girl with the type of headscarf the archetypal gypsy wears, and this girl was looking into a big dark blue glittery crystal ball of some sort. It looked a lot more interesting than the dolls Carly had been playing with, so she almost ripped the lid off the cardboard box and took out a crystal ball which looked exactly the same as the one on the box, and there were rings with magnets on them, that scarf the fortune-telling girl was wearing on the glossy box, an earring, a pack of Madame Rosa Fortune Teller cards, and an instruction handbook.

But there were no batteries! Carly felt like crying. She showed her father the toy crystal ball and asked him what type of batteries would fit it, and he said 'Ah, it takes two AA sized batteries. We'll get some when the shops open - after Boxing Day.'

'I can't wait that long, Dad,' Carly groaned, tugging at his knee as she knelt there with such a sorrowful look.

Mark looked at his son, who was eyeing the crystal ball with a sneer. 'I think your brother Mike has two AA batteries he could spare, don't you Mike?'

The boy shook his head.

'You do, in that electronic bowling game thingy,' Mark reminded his eldest son.

'No, I use that game,' Mike mumbled, and started unpacking his Nintendo.

'How could you forget to get batteries, Dad? This isn't fair!' Carly whined.

'I didn't get you that thing,' he said, looking at the Madame Rosa box, and he turned to his wife and asked: 'Did you get her that, love?'

Patsy shook her head and said, 'No. The tag'll say

who its from.'

Carly looked at the tag, but it merely said: 'To Carly' – and nothing else.

At this point there was a loud knock on the front door and Patsy went to answer it. It was her parents, and they had brought more presents for the family. Carly soon forgot about the Madame Rosa toy and went to her Nanna and Grandpa. They'd brought her a huge box containing some vintage doll collection, which Carly opened immediately, and then after the Christmas dinner, Carly's Nan, Agnes, saw the Madame Rosa Crystal Ball toy and said a curious thing which immediately caught Carly's imagination. 'I used to have a crystal ball which I looked into when I was just a bit older than you,' Agnes said, to which her daughter – Carly's mum (who'd had a bit too much sherry) said: 'I still have it up in the loft!'

'Oh, really?' Agnes asked, and Carly became so excited when she heard this.

'I'm not going up there to look for that if that's what you're thinking,' Carly's dad, Mark said, shaking his head.

'I'll look for it!' Carly volunteered.

'I don't need you to go and look for anything up there,' Patsy told her husband in a derisive tone. 'You put your foot through the ceiling of Mike's room last time you went up there,' Patsy reminded him as she got up off the sofa and went into the hallway.

'You always have to bring that up,' Mark's voice rose in pitch and then he followed his wife out of the living room. 'And by the way you're in no fit state to be climbing up ladders!'

But Patsy did go up the ladder into the loft, and as

well as locating the crystal ball of her mum's, which was wrapped in a dusty old black velvet cloth, she also brought down an old album full of Polaroid snaps and black and white photographs of family, friends, pets and neighbours. Mark cringed when Patsy opened the album and showed Carly an old picture of her father when he had just started courting Patsy.

But Carly was more interested in the crystal ball, and she watched her Nan clean it with a handkerchief. 'Can I see, Nan? Can I see, please?' Carly held out her little hands.

'Yeah, but watch you don't drop it through that, Carly,' Agnes said, looking at the smoked-glass top of the coffee table.

Carly held the clear ball and looked through it, and she saw the picture of the muted television upside down. 'What do you do to see things in it?' the girl asked, and Carly used the old black velvet cloth to instruct her. She spread it out on the coffee table, and then put the crystal ball in the centre of it. 'You look through the ball at the blackness of the cloth, and you relax, and some fortune tellers look past the ball – '

'I don't think it's a good idea to be teaching our daughter the Dark Arts,' Mark interrupted with a very concerned look in his wide eyes.

'It's harmless,' Patsy said, squeezing his hand, 'go one mum, show us how it's done.'

Agnes tried to reassure her worried son-in-law with a smile as she continued her scrying tutorial: 'You just stare into the ball, at the black cloth behind it and try and clear your mind, the way people who meditate do, and after a while you see images, and sometimes moving images and things. I used to visualise clouds parting, and then I'd see all kinds of things.'

'Dad!' Mike, the eldest son suddenly shouted from across the room. He'd been gazing out the window at a girl he had a crush on. 'The Reverend's coming down the path!'

Mark grabbed the crystal ball and the black cloth and wrapped it up and put it behind a scatter cushion on the sofa, just behind his wife.

Then there came a gentle knock, and Mike opened the door. The Reverend of the church the family attended called to tell them about a jumble sale he was arranging in a week's time. He was looking for old toys and volunteers to man the stalls. Mike gave the vicar some sherry and discussed the logistics of the jumble sale – as Carly sneaked her hand under the cushion and retrieved the crystal call. She then crept up to her room ever so quietly as everyone was distracted by the clerical guest.

In her bedroom, Carly spread the black velvet square of the cloth out on her duvet, and then she placed the old crystal ball in the centre of the cloth, and she did as her Nan had instructed. She relaxed and her eyes went a little out of focus as she fixed her attention on the dark cloth by gazing through the crystal sphere.

About a minute passed when Carly saw what she could only describe as dancing shapes of pale light in the orb – similar to the pattern sunlight produces on a wall or ceiling when it reflects off the water in a swimming pool. She saw a greyish face slowly materialise in the crystal ball – and it started off as an out-of-focus skull with dark sockets, and it rapidly condensed into a rather clear picture of a man she had never seen before. He had on a flat round hat, and she realised it was a soldier. Being so young, Carly did not know the hat worn by the eerie face in the crystal ball was called a 'kepi' – a hat most would associate with the French military and police uniforms. Carly was not aware that her Nan had obtained the crystal ball from an old French woman who had run a glorified junk shop in the East End of London in the 1930s. As Carly looked at the soldier in the peculiar hat she saw him screw his face up as if he was in pain, and then suddenly that face graphically 'came away' – the words Carly used to describe the soldier's face being blown off later on when she told her mother about the grisly vision.

The child recoiled in shock, and saw the face dissolve into an amorphous cloud which reminded the girl of a drop of milk 'blossoming' when it disperses in a glass of water. She then saw a beautiful foreign-looking woman – perhaps Spanish – with very dark eyes and a head of wavy black glossy hair, and she was talking, but Carly could not hear anything – she could just see the little lips in the image of the woman's face fluttering. That face then faded, and many more scenes came and went in the crystal ball, and Carly went downstairs with it, but the vicar was still there, and when she tried to mention what she had seen, her mum ushered her into the kitchen and said: 'Don't let the reverend see that ball; they don't allow things like that in the church. Put it away till he's gone.'

Carly went up to her room again with the ball, and began to practice scrying again. This time, something very exciting happened. Carly saw what seemed like an old public house interior, perhaps in Victorian or Edwardian times, with men in flat caps drinking, and most of them had moustaches. This time, though, the girl *heard* music which seemed to come from the crystal ball, and it sounded like a badly-tuned piano. It was a melody the child had never heard before, and the significance of the scene was – and still is – unknown. Then something took place which terrified Carly. She saw a pretty girl walking down a dark street. The girl looked achingly familiar to Carly, and as she walked along, Carly thought she could even hear the girl's heels on the pavement clacking away. Who *was* this girl, Carly asked herself, and then she realised that the young lady looked like a much younger version of her mother! The images all seemed to be monochrome, and of a pale greyish colour with poor washed-out contrast.

The girl who strongly resembled Patsy, Carly's mum, walked along and now she had her back to the crystal-gazer, and the image got smaller and smaller as she walked down what looked like a very long alleyway. Then the scene changed, and a young man with curly dark hair gazed out the crystal ball at Carly. His eyebrows were joined in the middle and he had a mole to the right side of his right eye. Carly sensed this man was bad. He covered the lower half of his face with a dark cloth, and then he turned that partially-obscured face left as he peeped around a corner. He was in the same alleyway Carly had just seen her mother walk down. He walked around that corner, and the 'eye' of the crystal ball followed him. He walked faster and faster and Carly could just about hear his feet softly padding for a while – but then she heard the click-clack of shoes – the shoes of the girl who looked like a young version of her mum. Then she saw the back of that young woman as she walked ahead of the man with the joined-up eyebrows. That woman was being followed by him, and she kept looking around – and then, he ran forward and grabbed her, and he slapped her face and pushed her against the wall. Carly saw him force himself on the woman, and was so upset by what she saw, she started to cry. She ran out the room, and as she did she heard a loud bang. It was the front door closing as the vicar left.

Carly ran down the stairs and ran across the hallway and into the living room. She threw herself onto her mother, who was seated on the sofa with a Martini in her hand, and the contents of the glass went all over Patsy's blouse.

'Carly! What the devil are you playing at?' she yelled, and Mark also berated her loudly.

'Mummy, I saw a horrible man attacking you!' Carly told her mother, and she buried her tearful face in her mother's bosom.

'What?' Patsy asked, pushing her daughter away slightly so she could hear what she was saying.

Carly told her mother exactly what she had seen, and the colour seemed to leave Patsy's face. What the girl said also seemed to strike some chord deep down in the memories of her grandparents, for they looked at one another, then looked at Mark.

'I told you not to let her mess with that crystal ball, didn't I?' Mark said to his wife - and he also directed his furious gaze to Agnes, and he shook his head as he turned the volume down on the TV with the remote.

'Did someone attack you, mummy? When you were young?' Carly asked, and she was greeted by a very telling silence.

'I'm throwing that thing out, now!' Mark got up and he left the room and went up to his daughter's room. There was no sign of the crystal ball or the black cloth anywhere. Mark heard his son Mike in his bedroom laughing and talking to his brother David as he had the ghetto blaster blaring. He went in there and asked his son's to keep the music down because Bernie was asleep, and then he asked if they had seen the crystal ball that Carly had been 'dicking about' with. The lads said they hadn't, and Mike then grumpily said something and slid the portable stereo's volume right down.

Mark went back downstairs and had it out with Carly. 'Alright, where have you put it, eh?' he asked.

'Put what?' the girl was baffled by the question.

'That crystal ball, that's what!'

'It's on my bed,' she told him.

'No, it's not!' Mark said through gritted teeth and then he noticed that his wife was in tears and his mother-in-law was offering her a handkerchief. 'See what you've done? Its supposed to be Christmas, and you've upset your mother.'

'I'm sorry,' Carly said, then started crying again, and her Nan opened her arms to the girl and she went to her for comfort.

'Where did you put that bloody crystal ball, Carly?' Mark asked, once again.

'She's just told you: it's on her bed!' Agnes told her son-in-law in an annoyed tone.

'But it *isn't*,' Mark replied, just as loud and aggravated as Agnes, 'and she *knows* where it is; she's hidden it.'

'I haven't! I left it on my bed,' Carly said, and then she turned to her sympathetic Nan and said, 'honest

Nan, I'm not hiding it.'

'It's alright, pet, *I* believe you,' she told her, then glared at Mark, who was stooping as he looked with great empathy into Patsy's face.

The next day, Carly was in her room, playing with the old-fashioned dolls when there was a knock at the front door of the house. She went out onto the landing and looked through the railings under the hand rail to see who it was. It was Terry, the next door neighbour who often went for a drink with her father. She quickly realised something about Terry which sent butterflies fluttering in her stomach. Although he was bald, he had patches of curly greying hair on each side of his head, but he had eyebrows that met in the middle – and *he had a mole at the side of his right eye* - just like the younger man she had seen assaulting her mother in the crystal ball. 'That's him,' Carly murmured to herself, and went all cold and clammy. She went downstairs and saw her father bringing cans of lager from the fridge to Terry, who was sitting on the sofa as he watched the telly. Carly went into her mother's bedroom, and there she found Patsy looking in the mirror of her dresser, applying make-up. She asked Carly what she wanted and told her she was getting ready to go to the pub for a Boxing Day drink. Mike would look after the house till they returned.

'Is Terry going with you and dad?' Carly asked.

'Yes, why?' Patsy asked her daughter.

'Mummy, that man I saw in the crystal ball – the one who attacked you – '

Patsy returned a shocked expression.

'It was *him* – Terry, only he had hair and he looked young, and I know its him because his eyebrows are sort of joined up and he has this mole at the side of his eye. He had something covering his face up to here – ' Carly pointed to the top of her nose, 'but I could tell it was him; he looked like the old black and white photograph in the album that her mother had shown her on Christmas Day.'

A tear trickled from Patsy's eye, and she hugged her daughter. And then, for some reason she left the bedroom and went downstairs, and there was a row. Carly heard her mum say she no longer wanted to go for a drink and she told Terry to go home because she didn't feel well.

That night, around 9pm, Carly was sitting in bed, sketching a princess in a drawing pad, when she was startled by the sudden appearance of the crystal ball and the black cloth spread out beneath it. The ball had literally appeared out of thin air and was resting on the duvet at the end of the bed. Carly stopped sketching and put her marker and pad down, and went to look at the weird orb. She touched it gently with her index finger, just to prove to herself that it was really there, that she was not imagining it or dreaming. It was there alright, but how? Where had it been for the past day and why was it back?

Carly looked about her quiet bedroom, understandably a little anxious, and she felt as if something – or someone – was toying with her – playing games.

She looked at the crystal ball and she felt as if she could not turn her eyes away from it; it felt as if that ball had some hypnotic hold over her. She sat there, and she knew she was going to see something – and she did. She saw that pretty girl again – the one she suspected of being her mum in her younger days – and now she could tell without a doubt that it was her mother; she looked a little older now, and she was in a bed, with a nurse standing by her. Then, all of a sudden, she heard a voice – a female voice – shout: 'Push!'

Simultaneously as Carly heard this word, she saw her mother's face close up, and she was clenching her teeth, and her eyes were squeezed shut. She seemed to be trying to do something and the sheer effort was showing in her face. At the time, Carly did not know that she was looking at her mother as she was in the throes of labour, having a baby. She heard that nurse saying: 'Push!' again and again and there were other figures about in the room, possibly medics, it was hard to say because they seemed out of focus – but the next scene was sharply in focus. In the crystal ball, Carly saw the scene change. Her mother and the nurse faded away, and she saw a woman with vivid red hair kissing a man who had her up against a tree. That man turned around, and Carly threw her hands to her face – because it was her father. He looked many years younger than he did now, but she could tell it was him. Then, all of a sudden, Carly heard the woman actually speak, and she said: 'I hardly know you. I met you today for the first time and here we are in the park, kissing and carryin' on, and your missus - who's my best mate - is in hospital havin' a kid. You're a right one you are.'

And that woman giggled and the man – who was undoubtedly Carly's father in his younger days – began to kiss her; *really* kiss her...her face...neck...cleavage...

Then the black cloth the crystal ball rested on

showed through, and blanked out the images. The visions had gone. Carly told her mother what she had seen on the following day when she was preparing the dinner while Mark was out having a drink. Patsy seemed very shocked at the mention of the red hair, and she said to her daughter, 'Wait there a minute, love.'

Patsy went and found that album she had brought down from the loft the day before and leafed through it. She pointed to the black and white photograph of a young woman – and Carly's jaw dropped. Although the picture was monochrome and colourless – she could tell it was that very same redhead she'd seen her dad kissing in the crystal ball. 'Who is she, mum?'

'When I was having Mike, in hospital love – you know, having a baby – that girl there in the photograph, was my best mate, Collette. Your dad had met her the day I was taken in to hospital with labour pains.'

Years later, when Carly was old enough - when she had been told the so-called facts of life, and when she was mature enough to be told about the unsavoury machinations of life and the complexity of human relationships - Patsy told her the whole truth. Carly's mother told her that she had been raped in her teens, and the man who had assaulted her was never identified because he had covered most of his face with a dark handkerchief. The despicable act had been carried out in an alleyway one night when Patsy had been returning home after a row with her boyfriend – Carly's future father. The identity of the rapist had been a mystery, and not knowing who had assaulted her had been an added torture to Patsy – but that day, when Carly had seen that man in the crystal ball carrying out the rape, and when she had told her mother the man had joined-up eyebrows and the telltale mole at the side of his eye – Patsy had realised who had raped her that night when she was just 19. She had confronted Terry a few days after that Boxing Day in 1988 and he had denied being the rapist and had even threatened to take legal action for defamation of character – but then he had committed suicide days later by hanging himself in a garage. Carly's husband had actually believed his friend – and had told Patsy that she had driven an innocent man to take his own life. Then Patsy confronted Mark and asked him if he'd had an affair with her best friend – Collette – while she was giving birth to his son. Mark had abreacted to the allegation and threatened to leave her, but he later admitted (when he was drunk) that he *had* 'been weak - but just once'.

By this time, when Patsy told Carly about the rape and Mark's affair, Agnes had passed on, and the significance of the visions of the Spanish woman, the piano being played in the pub, and the French solider remain unknown. Furthermore, after that evening on Boxing Day of 1988, Carly never again set eyes on the weird crystal ball.

THE LAST CHRISTMAS

In December 2010, the two-year-old marriage of Ryan, aged 30, and Taylor, aged 25, was at its rockiest, and in one week alone, he had threatened to leave her four times and she had attempted to leave him six times and had even hinted that she knew someone who'd 'do him in' if she merely texted him. The neighbours of the continually warring couple were compiling diaries of the disturbances to build a case for the serving of an ASBO. Where did it all go wrong for Ryan and Taylor? People close to the couple knew that, paradoxically, they loved one another, and they wanted nothing more than a family, but times were hard and money was hard to come by, and Taylor worked as a freelance cleaner, while Ryan worked part-time delivering prescriptions from a pharmacy. Taylor thought he should be doing more to bring in 'some megadough' as she called it, by moving to London and getting a job as a stockbroker. Ryan had once been a wizard with money and had worked in telesales a long time ago, and was known for being able to sell anything, but since his marriage, he had become rather depressed and lacking in self-confidence. Physically, he was a little man with a pot belly, receding hair, tortured into a peculiar comb-over, and seemed plagued with sciatica. Taylor was of an Amazonian build – but not overweight. She was a 'mesomorph', to use the scientific terminology, and perfectly proportioned in the eyes of Ryan. Facially she had prominent cheekbones and was not all that unlike the actress Jennifer Lawrence.

Christmas was coming and this was also putting some strain on the relationship, as Taylor had 9 nieces, five brothers, parents, grandparents, many close friends and of course, the in-laws, to get presents for, and Ryan had to buy his family, friends and relatives gifts as well, and there just wasn't enough money to go around at the moment. Ryan owed an awful lot of money to a certain well-known bank owned by a Spanish company, and most of their final demands went straight in the bin unopened. Ryan also had several rent arrears hanging over his head from the council flat he had lived in before he had even met his wife. He did the Lottery twice a week and had the occasional flutter on the horses (unknown to Taylor) every now and then but the gambling never paid off. Taylor also had debts with a certain popular clothing catalogue which had the worst customer services telephone service on earth.

And then, one morning, in the middle of a blazing row that should have been a pay-per-view event on WWE, Taylor's telephone rang and she released her hands from Ryan's throat as she lay on top of him and he stopped trying to bite her kneecap, which was pinning his right shoulder down.

Taylor didn't recognise the number on the iPhone's display and immediately thought it was the catalogue people calling about her eternal debt problem. She was ready to scream at them, the mood she was in. There was a pause, and then a well-spoken man said, 'Hello, may I talk to Taylor?' And he mentioned her surname of course.

'Speaking – who are you?'

'Marc Goldrain of Goldrain and Kreele, er – ' he replied, and he could hear she was panting, out of breath, and so he blushed and told her: 'I'm sorry if I interrupted you doing something, um – '

'Who *is* this?' Taylor shrieked, and got up off Ryan, who was curious to know who was calling, but he suspected it had something to do with the catalogue people.

'Marc Goldrain of Goldrain and Kreele, the solicitors – '

'I'm paying off as much as I can already! What more can I give? You'll be asking for my stem cells next!' Taylor growled, feeling so frustrated and humiliated.

Mr Goldrain gave a nervous laryngitic laugh. 'No, no, no, I'm not asking for money, I'm informing you that I need to talk to you at your convenience because there is something to your advantage which I must inform you of.'

'Can you say that in plain English please?' Taylor asked.

'Tell them to piss off!' Ryan said, leaning on his elbows as he looked up at his towering wife. 'You're paying them enough!'

Taylor gently kicked him in the crutch and waved her hand down at him, gesturing for him to be quiet.

'Someone has left something substantial to you,' Goldrain said with glee in his voice.

'I hope this isn't some trick to get me to accept a summons or something,' Taylor warned.

That afternoon, she and Ryan were sitting in the offices of Goldrain & Kreele Solicitors, and Marc Goldrain looked exactly as she imagined him from his voice on the phone: curly perm, over-tanned, wearing a pin-striped suit a size too small for him, and capped teeth with two massive maxillary central incisors like he'd come straight from Whoville. The top and bottom of it was that one Morven Beatty had left his house and its entire contents to Taylor in his last will and testament, and he had died a few weeks ago, aged 85. Taylor had cleaned his house for two years and found him to be a very strange old man with a pair of the warmest and expressive eyes she had ever seen. He had seemed to be carrying a lot of sorrow around, and Taylor wanted to ask him about his life but had always felt as if that would be getting a bit too personal. Why on earth had he left a house which – according to Mr Goldrain – was worth three-quarters of a million pounds? Ryan, being the perennial bad-minded paranoid skunk, wondered just *what* type of services Taylor had provided in addition to her cleaning routine, and his fevered imaginings included her feather duster.

It all seemed too good to be true. The couple only had to sell the house now and their debts would be cleared and they could face Christmas with a smile for the first time in so many years. All of the forms were signed by Taylor, and she had a sneaking suspicion that some relative of Morven Beatty would be in touch to claim a share of the house and its contents. Taylor expressed these fears to Marc Goldrain, and he assured her that there were no relatives. Mr Beatty's wife Paulette had died many years ago, and the son of the couple had been knocked down and killed in a car accident when he was only five.

The amazing gift of such an expensive house in the reserved suburbs did not make the marriage of Ryan and Taylor any less rocky though. Taylor wanted to stay in the house after discovering that the furniture and original oil paintings were worth nearly £70,000 – more than enough to start a new life free of debt without selling the house. Ryan thought she was crazy and said that he might divorce her and claim half of the value of the house, to which she threatened to knock him out.

Just a few days before Christmas, a violent row broke out in the house, and Ryan yelled: 'Sell this house or I am leaving you for good! And I mean it Tay! And remember that if I go out that door you will never find anyone out there as loving and genuine *and* as understanding as me! The only fellahs you'll get will be gold-diggers!'

'Look at the state of you,' Taylor said calmly, walking around him, circling him like a lion about to pounce on an anorexic antelope. 'You're all comb-over and paranoia!'

'You always bring that up, don't you, eh?' he said, pointing to his ear to ear hairstyle. 'They recognise racism in this world, and god help anyone who calls someone fat, but people think its okay to mention a comb-over – something I can't help!'

'But its true,' she told him with a wicked grin, 'you've got a comb-over from Hell!'

'And what about your make up, eh? Make up is a comb-over for the skin! And you have eyebrows like the Hulk but you pluck them all out and draw little ones you'd rather have with a pencil – and everyone can see they're just *drawn* on, ha-ha!'

That killed the smile on her face. 'That's not cricket; not cricket at all,' was her bizarre reply to Ryan's close to the marrow critique. She looked around for something to throw at him as if she was merely searching for the TV remote. This was the final straw, criticising her eyebrows.

He sensed he was in deep trouble now, and desperately tried to back-pedal: 'But I still love the bones of you, no matter what your eye –'

She picked up a marble bust of Beethoven from the sideboard. Now, this bust was almost life-sized and weighed a whopping ten-and-a-half kilograms, and yet Taylor hurled it in an amazing curved trajectory towards Ryan's head like that kilted Highlander Putting the Shot on the famous box of porridge oats.

Ryan ducked and Beethoven sailed past him, missing him by millimetres – and impacted into the wall, dislodging wallpaper and plasterboard.

'You're insane!' Ryan screeched, looking at the damage to the wall and the fragments of Beethoven lying on the floor behind him.

Taylor burst into tears and rushed towards him, and before Ryan could flee she as giving him a bear hug as her tears went down his back. 'I'm sorry! I'm sorry!' she said over and over. 'You're hair's perfect,' she said, sounding muffled because her lips were squashed against the base of his neck.

When they had both calmed down, Ryan noticed something quite odd. In the large crack in the wall he could see a wooden green door showing through. He pointed it out to Taylor and they rapped their knuckles on the wall and discovered that there was a door there behind the wall.

Ryan then paced up and down the parlour and then he went outside.

'Where are you going?' Taylor asked him.

Ryan went outside and walked around the house, and noticed something he'd not noticed before; there was an unaccounted for cube-shaped area of the building on the ground floor, apparently lying adjacent to the parlour and kitchen. He had never noticed this mysterious extra area before because the two walls of its corner were covered in ivy and bordered with tall hedges. He could see where the window of what must be a hidden room had been bricked up and rendered a long time ago by the looks of it.

'What are you looking at?' Taylor queried with an annoyed look. 'Stop being so mysterious.'

'There's a secret room in this house,' Ryan told her, and went back indoors and showed her where it was. 'That entire wall of the parlour there is one side of the hidden room, and that door you can see through the crack must have given access to it at one time.'

'You're not going to get into it are you?' Taylor asked her husband, knowing what the answer would be. He was a very curious man by nature.

'We should see what's in there, Tay,' Ryan started to pull bits of plaster off with his bare hands.

'Well we should get someone in to do that,' Taylor gently tapped his hands as he tried to pull more plasterboard away. 'You can't knock a nail straight, Ryan; I'm not having you knocking down a supporting wall.'

He turned to face her with a right sour face. 'You

always knock me down, don't you? Always belittling me – '

'Oh don't start all that wallowing in self-pity,' she said, talking over him, 'I'm just saying you are absolutely shit at DIY and you could destroy this house.'

But somehow he convinced her that he could perform the relatively easy task of exposing a door that was merely 'hidden by a few millimetres of wallpaper and plasterboard' – and by the next day, in the afternoon, Ryan proudly showed her the green door. The keyhole to the door had been blocked with plaster, and so, Taylor suggested getting a professional locksmith out to open it – but Ryan couldn't help himself; the curiosity had consumed him by now and he ached to know what lay beyond the door. When Taylor was getting a bath she heard the whine of an electric drill, and she swore as she hauled herself out of the bath. With just a towel wrapped around her torso she went downstairs and saw Ryan forcing the green door open just as she set foot in the parlour.

He turned when he heard her bare wet feet padding across the carpet.

'I'm gonna kill you Ryan! You said you were going to wait till tomorrow to get a locksmith!'

'Its open now, calm down,' her impatient husband said, and he yanked the door open.

What felt like a blast of sweet air hit the couple, blowing Ryan's comb-over so it was left dangling from the right side of his head. Taylor dropped the towel in shock from the blast.

'What the hell was that?' Ryan wiped his hair back across the top of his head and ventured into the secret room. Taylor followed close behind, naked as the day she was born. Ryan's hand searched for a switch on the wall – and found one. It felt round and hard, like the old bakelite switches of long ago. He clicked it and a dim bulb hanging from the ceiling lit up the room, revealing a very strange interior. It was like a time capsule of a living room of over fifty years ago. There was an old *Radio Times* magazine draped over the arm of an old-fashioned armchair, and in the corner was a quaint Christmas tree rigged with coloured light bulbs; not LEDs, but real filament bulbs, and the wire connecting them was thick, brown and twisted. There was an antique television on a table in the corner, and Taylor looked at the ceiling and saw the vintage decorations made of crepe, foil and coloured paper.

'Wednesday, 25 December, 1957,' Ryan said, stooping to read the date on the *Radio Times*.

'It's like the room has been left the way it would have been on Christmas Day,' Taylor said softly, looking about. She left the room to grab the towel to cover herself and returned. She and Ryan looked at everything in this mini-museum of the 1950s.

The fairy lights on the tree came on.

'Whoa!' Taylor recoiled in shock and looked at Ryan's hands, then to his face.

'I didn't do it!' he said, then something caught his attention, and Taylor followed his line of eyesight to see what it was. It was the old fashioned television set. The screen was starting to glow as a picture came on. A choir of voices emanated from it, and they were singing *God Save the Queen*.

A black and white scene came into focus on the screen of the old thick cathode ray tube – a panning shot of some old building, and then a lady appeared in the next scene, a young woman. It was the young Queen Elizabeth II – The Queen.

'Happy Christmas,' she said, 'Twenty-five years ago, my grandfather broadcast the first of these Christmas messages…'

'The Queen's Christmas Speech,' Ryan said with a slight grin. 'She looks like a kid.'

'Isn't this creepy?' Taylor said, and Ryan saw her shudder.

'Paulette!' said a voice behind the couple, and Taylor swung around and yelped. Ryan turned slowly, somehow knowing there was something supernatural there.

A man of about thirty, perhaps a little older, stood there, with a boy of about five by his side. The man had his hair slicked back with oil or Brylcreem and he wore a white shirt and blue tie and a green woollen cardigan. His trousers were wide and sharply pleated, and Ryan noticed the highly polished brogues on his feet. The boy was sandy-haired and had big sad eyes, and he wore a red pullover, chocolate brown shorts, red socks and black shoes.

'Oh mummy, you came back!' the little boy said, and the love in his eyes was phenomenal – they seemed to glow with affection.

He ran towards Taylor, and before she could think of running away from that room, the boy had run into her, and for some strange reason, she found herself picking him up. Ryan looked at her with an expression of total shock, because now his wife was changing before his eyes. Her hair had become shoulder length and blonde, and she was wearing a pink billowy skirt with white polka dots and she had a tiny waist secured with a belt. The blouse she wore was white and looked as if it was made of satin. Taylor's face seemed to be changing before Ryan's startled eyes. Her nose looked as if it was turned up now, and her eyes were becoming darker and almond shaped.

'I missed you mummy!' the boy clung to Taylor and she hugged him back hard and patted his back as she said, 'And I missed you.' The voice was not that of Taylor, but of someone rather well-spoken, and this really unnerved her husband.

'Taylor, put him down,' Ryan said, confused, 'he's not your kid!'

The whole room seemed to be lit up by an arc light now, and it no longer looked dusty and unlived in. 'Don't go away again, mummy!' the emotional boy in Taylor's arms said, and he burst into tears as she hugged him and said, 'There, there,' as she patted his back. Ryan noticed that the hand patting the boy's back no longer wore his wedding ring – but another style of ring instead. Ryan grabbed the little boy by the waist and pulled him away from Taylor, and the child let out a terrible loud scream.

'Leave him alone!' said the ghostly man behind Ryan, 'Leave him with mummy!'

'No!' cried Ryan, and he wrenched the child from the transformed Taylor and he kicked his little legs about furiously. 'You're not her son!' Ryan almost threw the child onto the sofa.

'Leave him with his mummy!' said the tall ghost in the cardigan, and he started to walk towards Ryan.

'Leave my child alone you monster!' Taylor screamed, and Ryan grabbed her by the hand and started to drag her out of that haunted room. He passed the weird man in the cardigan with the slicked back hair and noticed he was grinning as he stood there, watching Ryan trying to claim back his wife.

As soon as Ryan dragged Taylor out of that room, he saw that she was naked, and her towel was at her feet. Her hairstyle, eyes and face had reverted to normal, and the polka dot dress and blouse had vanished. The ground shook, as if an earthquake was striking the foundations of the house, but when it faded away, Ryan noticed that the ghostly man had gone.

The couple were so scared by their experience, they sat in their car for a while with the heater on and discussed if they should leave the place or not.

Taylor said she had felt an immense love for that little ghostly boy – as if it had been her own son, and she had realised that the man standing at the door had been the young ghost of Morven Beatty – the old man who had left the house to her.

'We should give the place another chance, and if anything strange happens, we should sell it and move on,' Taylor proposed.

Ryan reluctantly agreed, and he and Taylor had the room sealed up again, but not long after this, the couple began to hear strange noises coming from that hidden room. In the middle of the night they heard what sounded like 1950s songs coming from an old radio or record player in the forgotten room, and sometimes the sounds of a boy sobbing. In the end the ghostly goings-on proved too much for the couple and they sold the house and moved miles away. One strange side-effect of the haunting was that it cemented the relationship of the couple, and their arguments and rows became infrequent. After Taylor gave birth to a baby girl in 2012, the couple's relationship improved further, and nowadays Taylor and Ryan are like the archetypal Darby and Joan, and seem very content with one another. I researched this strange case and discovered that Taylor bore a slight resemblance to Mr Beatty's wife, Paulette, who died from after a short illness on Christmas Day – 1957. That last Christmas with his beloved wife, and the child he would soon lose in a road accident, was left like a time capsule when Mr Beatty had the room sealed up for posterity. Perhaps Mr Beatty left his house to Taylor because his cleaner reminded him of someone he had once loved – and lost.

Printed in Great Britain
by Amazon